You Go Girl London

Library of Congress Control Number: 2005907144

To order additional copies, please contact us.
BookSurge, LLC
www.booksurge.com
1-866-308-6235
orders@booksurge.com

YOU GO GIRL LONDON

A Travel Guide Just For The Girls

POLLY BOLINE
AND BARB CHESLEY

This Book Is Dedicated To Our Parents, Russ And Ruth Person.
Their Love Of Travel And Adventure Inspired Our Journeys.
To Our Husbands, Dave Boline And Joe Chesley, Who Encouraged
Us To Follow Our Dreams.

ACKNOWLEDGMENTS

We gratefully acknowledge the many people who helped with the creation of our book. We would especially like to thank our families: Dave, Katie and Jake Boline; and Joe, Joey, Sarah and Megan Chesley. Thank you for allowing us the time to write, research and travel. Without your computer expertise and assistance, we would still be searching for Word.

Karen Ylinen, our friend, editor, photographer and our You Go Girl London "guinea pig". Without your meticulous editorial skills our book would be just a mishmash of words. We can never repay you for the endless hours that you spent toiling over our numerous manuscripts. We will always lovingly refer to you as our "Queen Mum". Cheers Mish.

We would like to thank Philippa Gregory. *The Other Boleyn Girl* inspired us to go beyond the pages, and was the catalyst for our book. Your endorsement not only validated our work, but touched our hearts.

Don Huff's expert map and cover designs fulfilled all our dreams. To us, your illustrations are worthy of another Pulitzer Prize.

For their professional contributions and advice we would like to thank the following:

Joanna Allen (Visit Britain), Val Austin (Visit Britain) Bruce Bortz (Literary Attorney), Brett Dolman (Collections Curator, Tower of London & Hampton Court), Miss Christine Reynolds (Assistant Keeper of the Muniments, Westminster Abbey Library) and Natasha Woollard (P.R. Manager Tower of London).

For their support, encouragement and friendship:

Charlie and Terrie Allen, Sue Bermel, Ann Boline, Jen Bunce, Jodi Billman, Quinette Cook, Cheryl Engelman, Kandi Engelmann, Caroline and Eric Ethington, Caroline Gilmer, Lynn Garner, Judy Hoy, Kris Johnson, Michele Matthews, Tracy and Doug Moran, Linda Moreno, Jill Porter, Dave Person, Lynn Person, Cathy and Bill Salinger, Julie Semrau, Joanie Smith, Sherry and Jim Smith, Mike Ylinen, The Yet To Be Named Book Club and the many others that helped us with our journey.

CONTENTS

INTRODUCTION

As traveling sisters, we treasure our trips abroad. There's nothing like it; we can linger at the museums, catch a play, unwind at a pub or "shop 'til we drop". What we do on our girl getaways is up to us. We leave our husbands, children, jobs and cares behind, and have the time of our lives. London is one of our favorite spots; we have been there countless times and are familiar with the sights that appeal to women. The idea for *You Go Girl-London* came from a combination of our love of reading and travel. When we travel abroad, we find our experience richer when we link books with our journeys. As we trace the lives of the figures in the novels we read, the sights become more fascinating. We've included a list of our favorite books that we believe will enhance your travels. If you are involved in a book club, we hope *You Go Girl-London* will inspire your group to go beyond the pages and plan an incredible journey to London with just "the girls." Or grab your best friend, sister or mom and start planning! You'll never regret it. As traveling sisters we've had a blast and every trip has been an unforgettable adventure.

Big Ben

London is an expensive city, but we have found ways to make it affordable. You may think that a trip to London is a luxury beyond your reach and too extravagant. We are from middle class families, financing college tuition, school sports and children's car expenses; however, we always find incredible bargains and manage to work trips abroad into our budget. By using off-season travel, discount travel websites and frequent flyer programs, we have made our London trips a reality. During the off-season, we find the crowds are low, the hotel and airline costs are at bargain rates and the weather is often pleasant. Although weather is often an unpredictable factor when you travel, a rainy day in London is always preferred to an ordinary day at home!

This guidebook will easily slip into your purse and it is filled with all the information you will need to have a fantastic time in London. If you want to go to Westminster Abbey, shop at Harrods or maybe even check out the half-price theatre tickets at Leicester Square, we'll point you in the right direction. If you're a Beatle fan, we've mapped out a tour that will take you "Here, There and Everywhere," so practice that Beatle scream! We loved Princess Diana and include many sights that were meaningful in her life, as well as her memorials. There is also a wealth of Tudor history throughout London, and you'll soon be caught up in the "free reign" of Henry VIII, as well as his three offspring that inherited the throne. The Tower, Windsor Castle, and Hampton Court are filled with fascinating Tudor history, so make sure you read some of our recommended books before you go. There are also fabulous museums and galleries throughout London, and remember you're with the girls, so take your time and enjoy! When hunger strikes, there are so many choices that you're sure to find a great spot to eat on your own. However, we included our absolute favorite places to eat, just in case you're in the neighborhood. Look at our insider tips to help you plan your journey and navigate your way around London.

We've had so many fun and memorable experiences in London that we thought it might be fun to include a few in the book. Soon you'll be creating memories of your own. There's nothing like traveling with the girls, especially in "Swinging London." Be prepared to stir up that inner girl and have the time of your life! You Go Girl...Cheers!

HOW TO BOOK YOUR TRIP

There are plenty of travel bargains out there, but it is up to you to find them. By using the following websites you'll be able to find affordable airfare, hotels or package deals that will have you "over the pond" in no time. We'll help you narrow down your hotel choices to areas that are safe, reasonably priced and easily accessible to all the sights. So, have your passport ready to take advantage of all these super deals!

Major Airline Websites—The latest offers on both airfare and air and hotel packages can be found on every major airline website. Be sure to get on e-mail lists for specials. Each airline has ways to accumulate miles toward discounted or free trips; we like to think of these as You Go Girl miles! In order to accumulate miles, you must enroll in a frequent flyer program, which is free of charge. Besides flying on the airline, you can also accumulate miles with credit cards that can be either airline specific or offer miles that can be used toward any airline. These cards usually carry higher interest rates, so we recommend they be paid off in their entirety each month (tip—most college tuition can be paid by credit card). Check your airline websites for other ways to earn miles, such as hotel stays, car rental and telephone specials. As a rule, most airlines require 50,000-60,000 miles for a free European trip. Some airlines offer cash and miles programs. Believe it or not, we each flew from the Midwest to Paris in late February for 10,000 miles and $200 each, including all taxes. If we had chosen London, it would have been a few dollars more because taxes are higher. We jumped on this special even though we had just gone on a London-Paris excursion three months earlier. Sometimes the deals are too good to resist!

American Airlines: www.aa.com

British Airways: www.britishairways.com

Continental Airlines: www.continental.com

Delta: www.delta.com

Icelandair: www.icelandair.com
Departs from Minneapolis/St. Paul, Baltimore/Washington D.C., New York, Boston, San Francisco and Orlando.

Northwest Airlines: www.nwa.com

United Airlines: www.united.com

US Airways: www.usairways.com

Virgin Atlantic Airlines: www.virgin-atlantic.com
Virgin offers departures from New York City, Miami, Orlando, San Francisco, Washington D.C., Las Vegas and Boston.

Hotels—It can be overwhelming to pick a hotel from the thousands of choices in London. When looking for a hotel, it is important to look at its location, cost, amenities and proximity to transportation.

There are three main areas in London that contain the majority of affordable hotels: the West End, south of Hyde Park and north of Hyde Park. Of course there are many other sections, but we've found these to be safe and also convenient to the sights. Each area has its own distinct characteristics and charm that will appeal to the uptown girl, shopaholic or country girl.

The West End is considered to be the heart of London. This area runs roughly from Trafalgar Square in the south, north to Bloomsbury and west to Hyde Park. The West End is a very urban part of town, filled with theatres and shopping. Generally more expensive hotels are found here in relation to the other two areas we mention.

South of Hyde Park includes Kensington, South Kensington and Knightsbridge. This area includes many museums, upscale residential areas and shopping. We have stayed at a hotel next to the Gloucester Road tube stop and found it to be a nice area where you can find many restaurants, internet cafes, shops and grocery stores.

North of Hyde Park is a mixture of commercial and residential areas. We have stayed at numerous hotels that are located within blocks of Lancaster Gate tube stop. We enjoy having the parks across the street; they offer an oasis from the hustle and bustle of the city. There are a wide range of hotels in this area, the more upscale running from Lancaster Gate to the Marble Arch. The area around Bayswater and Notting Hill is where you will find the cheapest hotels, but this section is somewhat run down and we suggest you avoid this area when booking a hotel.

Hotel rooms in Europe are usually smaller and more expensive compared to American hotels. Hotels are given a star rating from one to five, with five stars being the best. Accommodations are usually for single (one person) or double (two people), but some offer triple (three people) and quad (four people). Trust us, the rooms will only accommodate the number of people that they recommend; also very strict fire codes regulate the number of people that can occupy a room. It's not like the states where you can pile a bunch of girls in one room and split the cost. Fabulous deals are available during the off-season, so don't rule out the higher-end hotels. We have found that, with research, you can stay at a four-star hotel for a three-star price. Off-season prices begin in October and continue through April. Generally, the lowest prices run from November through March, with the exception of the Christmas and New Year's holiday season.

Hotel amenities vary widely; check the website to see what is offered in the hotel. Some important items to check include:

- coffee makers in the room (this is vital for us)
- continental breakfast
- mini-fridge (we buy snacks such as yogurt and cheese that we store there)
- some hotels have 120 volt outlets, so there is no need for electrical converters

Look at the amenities to see if they have the ones that you consider important.

Proximity to a tube stop (subway system, also called the underground) is very important as this will be your main mode of transportation. We have always booked hotels within a few blocks from the underground. The hotel website should list the distance to the nearest underground.

Your most valuable tool when booking your hotel is www.tripadvisor.com. We love this free site; it gives impartial reviews of hotels from guests who have stayed there. It offers insight on location, cleanliness and value. The guests really tell it like it is, and soon you will be privy to all the good, bad, and ugly hotels throughout London. We personally use this site before booking **any** hotel in London. After reading a few reviews, we guarantee you will use this site too. These are a few excerpts from actual reviews sent into TripAdvisor regarding different hotel stays in London.

- The bathroom toilet had its seat hanging off of it and didn't flush properly, a sink that leaked nonstop and a shower with non-working doors and broken tile. We requested another room and were told that we had one of their best rooms.
- It was our first trip to England and after reading many hotel reviews took a chance that this hotel would meet our standards. We were delighted!
- We spent 7 nights there and were in complete misery...
- Great location. Good restaurants around the corner. Excellent breakfast...
- Booked on a last minute deal and was pleasantly surprised...
- The hotel room was so tiny and hot (even with a window open, fan running and temps of 70 degrees). The bathroom was smaller than one found in a camper and sink was the size of a small bowl. I would not recommend this hotel to anyone.

We have been lucky enough to stay in some very nice London hotels at a great price, but we did our homework! We want you to have a wonderful experience too, so please use TripAdvisor when booking a hotel. Maybe you'll want to add your own comments after your visit.

Hotels Only Websites—If you've found a great airfare and just need to book a hotel, try these sites. Once you've found a hotel that fits your needs, enter the hotel's name in a search engine such as www.google.com, to find additional prices on your hotel to comparison shop. Remember to check www.tripadvisor.com for reviews on your hotel before you actually book.

Go Hotels: www.gohotels.com

Hotels.com: www.hotels.com

Hotels-Europe WS: www.hotels-europe.ws.com

London Nights: www.londonnights.com

Grange Hotels: www.grangehotels.com

Holiday Inn: www.holiday-inn.com

Apartment Rental (London Flats) – For those of you who require a little more room or have a large group, renting a flat might be the way to go. It is often cheaper than a hotel room, and offers the advantages of a kitchen and other amenities. These are just a few of the many websites that offer apartment rental.

London Vacation Apartments: www.london-vacation-reservations.com

Your Stay: www.yourstay.com

Slow Travel U.K and Ireland: www.slowtrav.com

Manors: www.londonapartment.co.uk

Package Deals—Here is a list of sites that offer package deals to London. Our average London package has cost us about $125 per day for air, hotel and breakfast. Most packages are from five to seven days; although we have found that five days is sufficient for a taste of London, seven is ideal.

Go-today: www.go-today.com
Travel offered from most cities in the United States with combination air and hotel or just hotel. We have used this site and were pleased with the service.

Gate 1 Travel: www.gate1travel.com
Travel offered from New York City with combination air and hotels or just hotels.

Expedia: www.expedia.com
Travel offered from most cities with combination air and hotel packages; also offers both air and hotel separately.

Orbitz: www.orbitz.com
Travel offered from most cities with combination air and hotel packages; also offers air and hotel separately.

1-800-FlyEurope: www.1800flyeurope.com
Travel available from most cities for air and hotel packages; also offers both air and hotel separately.

AARP: www.aarp.org
If you are a member of AARP, you are eligible for discounted airline travel and packages. To become a member, you must be 50 years or older and pay a modest membership fee.

Travelzoo: www.travelzoo.com
Travelzoo lists sales and specials from over 300 companies.

Be sure to check your local travel agencies for specials and get on their e-mail list.

Passport—We both laugh when we look at our own passport pictures, but you need one of these flattering IDs to travel overseas. If you do not have a passport, apply for one as soon as you can since it can take up to six weeks to receive it. In order to take advantage of some of the best travel deals, it is important to have your passport ready. For more information, refer to www.state.gov/ and click on Travel and Living Abroad.

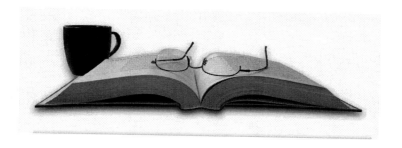

BOOKS THAT WE RECOMMEND

On our first trip to London we saw all the major attractions, but knew little about the history behind them. We had a wonderful trip and enjoyed our adventure. A few years later, we read *The Other Boleyn Girl* and became captivated by the Tudor monarchy. We went back and saw London in a whole new light; instead of just visiting landmarks, we relived history. Everything became more vivid when we visualized the people we had read about. Reading is one of our passions and we believe the books we've selected will spark your interest. If you're like us, you'll be intrigued by London's history before your feet actually hit the pavement. We highly recommend you read at least a few of our selections to make the most out of your trip. Our suggested reading covers a wide range of books, from a light read to more in-depth material. We offer a very brief description of each book, but for a more detailed review, visit www.amazon.com.

Tudor Period (1485-1603)

The Tudors were a family of which any soap opera would be proud. **Henry VIII** and his clan create a court full of lust, adulterous affairs, power struggles, murder, and political upheaval to keep any reader riveted. In the realm of **King Henry VIII**, few are far from the block and axe, including his close advisors, friends and even his queens. Following **Henry's** death, his children continue the unbelievable saga, beginning with the boy-king **Edward**, followed by the reign of **Bloody Mary**, and ending with the savvy **Queen Elizabeth I**. You will be fascinated with our selection of page-turners.

The Other Boleyn Girl by Philippa Gregory

A must read! This historical-fiction novel follows the lives of the Boleyn children, Mary, George, and Anne. The story is written from the point of view of Mary Boleyn who was Henry VIII's mistress. This book is a great choice for a book club. If you can read only one book before your journey, make it this one. (672 pages)

The Autobiography of Henry VIII: With Notes by his Fool, Will Somers: A Novel by Margaret George

Henry VIII's journal is found by his fool, Will Somers. The diary tracks Henry's life from early childhood to adulthood. This historical-fiction novel traces Henry's life from his perspective along with further insights from the fool. Although this is a very long book, we highly recommend it as it is very absorbing and moves quickly. (939 pages)

Mary Queen of France by Jean Plaidy

An entertaining light read that follows the life of Henry VIII's youngest sister, Mary. She is a strong-willed woman living in chauvinistic times and determined to get her way. Jean Plaidy wrote many romance-style books that cover the Tudors. If you like this style of writing, look for other books written by Jean Plaidy or under her pen names of Victoria Holt or Philippa Carr. (287 pages)

The Queen's Fool by Philippa Gregory

This book combines the fictional life of Hannah Green, a young Jewish girl, and the real lives of Henry VIII's children. When Hannah's "gift of sight" is revealed, she is brought to court to serve as a fool. Her service draws her into the dangerous intrigues of the royal family and her hidden life. The fascinating Dr. John Dee is one of the real-life characters introduced in this fast-paced novel. (512 pages)

The First Elizabeth by Carolly Erickson

After reading *The Other Boleyn Girl*, we became intrigued about what happened to the daughter of Henry VIII and Anne Boleyn. Although this is a biography, this book reads as a novel. It's a captivating read that includes all the details in a way that makes this book hard to put down. (407 pages)

My Enemy the Queen by Victoria Holt

This novel shows the life of Elizabeth I as seen through the eyes of her cousin, Lettice Knollys. Their lives intertwine when they battle over the two men they both love, Robert Dudley and Robert Devereux. (441 pages)

The Virgin's Lover by Philippa Gregory

The story begins when the young Elizabeth inherits the throne. The plot revolves around the love triangle between Elizabeth I, Robert Dudley and his wife Amy. (438 pages)

Behind the Mask: the life of Queen Elizabeth I by Jane Resh Thomas

If you don't want to spend a lot of time reading but want to know Queen Elizabeth's history, this is the book for you. It was written as a book for young people, but is better suited for adults. This book is a well-written, informative look into the life of Queen Elizabeth I, easy and enjoyable to read. (180 pages)

Tudors to the extreme—The following books are for the over-achievers who need to know every detail of the lives of the Tudors:

The Six Wives of Henry VIII by Alison Weir

Detail, detail, detail! Weir masterfully describes the Tudor times, the monarchy of Henry VIII, and takes an in-depth look at each of his six wives. (643 pages)

The Wives of Henry VIII by Antonia Fraser

Fraser is a stickler for meticulous research and detail; the author accurately portrays the mindset of King Henry VIII and his six very different queens. (496 pages)

The Children of Henry VIII by Alison Weir

The Tudor monarchy continues after the death of Henry VIII, with his heirs Edward, Mary, Elizabeth and his niece Jane vying for the crown. Weir again is fastidious in her research and delivers an enjoyable read. (400 pages)

I, Elizabeth by Rosalind Miles

This novel is written from Elizabeth's point of view, describing her feelings during the incredible events that shaped her life. (641 pages)

Princess Diana

From the moment we were introduced to Diana as the fiancé of Prince Charles, we became fascinated with her. We watched her grow from a shy, young girl into a strong woman who wasn't afraid to take on the British Monarchy. The following books offer deeper insight than the tabloids on this complex woman.

Diana: Her Story by Andrew Morton

In 1992, Morton wrote the book that rocked the Monarchy. It was written in secret collaboration with Diana. The frustration that Diana felt, trapped in a loveless marriage with all the restraints of being a Royal, is apparent in this book. (432 pages)

A Royal Duty by Paul Burrell

As footman to Queen Elizabeth II, butler to both the Prince and Princess of Wales, and finally, as Diana's personal butler, Paul Burrell offers a fascinating look into the lives and relationships of the Royals. Paul's book is a must-read for anyone interested in this intriguing family. (405 pages)

The Day Diana Died by Christopher Andersen

This book tastefully covers Diana's last days and her funeral. Anderson covers these events in a detailed and captivating way, reliving the day of her tragic death. (329 pages)

The Beatles

For many of us, the Beatles' songs played in the background of our lives. The memories of where we were and who we were with are as imbedded in our minds as the lyrics to their songs. For those of us who are die-hard fans as well as those who don't know much about the Fab Four, the following books are great reads:

The Beatle's Anthology by The Beatles

This book was written by Paul, George and Ringo with John's point of view taken posthumously from broadcasts and print. This beautiful coffee table book with pictures and text will keep a Beatle's fan occupied for days. (368 pages)

The Beatles by Hunter Davies

This book follows the Beatles from their childhood to the height of their popularity. Davies spent a year living and traveling with The Beatles and gives a wonderful insight into their lives. (377 pages)

Related Material

The Da Vinci Code by Dan Brown

This is a fast-paced novel that combines mystery and religion. It follows Robert Langdon and Sophie Neveau as they race through Paris and London to solve the secrets of the Priory of Sion and the Holy Grail. A sure winner that can cause people to question what they believe. *The Da Vinci Code* is an excellent book club choice. (454 pages)

Shakespeare, Dickens and Jane Austen

These three authors are synonymous with British literature. We haven't recommended any books selections due to the limited sights that pertain to these authors within London. Although we haven't included their books, we've listed the few sights we've found and the movies that they've inspired.

MOVIES

For those of you who might not have the time to read, but still want to get the flavor of London, here is a selection of our favorite chick flicks, classics and even a little Beatlemania. Hop into your jammies, pop some popcorn, open a bottle of wine and enjoy. This is also another good excuse for a girls' night out!

Oliver
A Christmas Carol
Shakespeare in Love
Romeo and Juliet
Sense and Sensibility
Emma
Bridget Jones's Diary
Love Actually
A Hard Day's Night
Help
The Full Monty
Finding Neverland
Notting Hill
Hook
Calendar Girls
Concert for George

TUDOR HISTORY

When **Edward IV** died in 1485, there had been 85 years of civil war in England. He was of the House of York, its symbol the white rose. They were at war with the Lancastrians's whose symbol was the red rose; hence the War of the Roses.

Edward V was proclaimed King of England at age 12, following his father's death. **Edward IV** had named his brother, **Richard** as **Edward V's** protector until **Edward** was old enough to rule on his own. **Richard** had other ideas and he promptly had young **Edward** and his only brother taken to the Tower. They were never seen alive again (the bodies of two small boys were later unearthed at the Tower). **Richard** quickly declared himself **King Richard III**.

The Lancastrians leader was **Henry Tudor**. He led his men to battle against **Richard III** at Bosworth. **Henry's** troops were triumphant and **Henry** became **King Henry VII**. **Henry VII** married **Edward V's** sister, **Elizabeth of York**, combining the two warring factions and their symbols into the Tudor rose (the York white rose upon the Lancastrian red).

Henry VII and his wife had four children. **Arthur**, the eldest and heir to the throne was a sickly youth. His brother **Henry**, the spare, was robust, smart and handsome. **Margaret**, their eldest daughter, was married to **James IV of Scotland** and became the grandmother of **Mary, Queen of Scots**. The baby of the family was **Mary**, who like her brother **Henry**, was smart, attractive and full of spirit. **Henry** and **Mary** were very close.

Arthur was pledged to marry **Catherine of Aragon, Princess of Spain**, uniting the two countries against their common enemy, France. The wedding took place when he was 15 and she was 16. It was a short marriage; **Arthur** was dead within three months due to sweating sickness.

Arthur's brother, **Henry**, became heir to the throne. **Henry VII** died in 1509, making **Henry VIII** King of England when he was only 18 years old. **Henry VIII** promptly married his dead brother's wife, **Catherine of Aragon**. For them to marry, they needed and got permission from the Pope. Their court was full of banquets and jousts.

Henry's best friend, **Charles Brandon**, was **Henry's** equal in sports and they competed in wrestling, jousts and hunting. **Henry's** youngest sister, **Mary**, fell in love with **Charles**. This didn't fit in with **Henry's** plan for his sister; besides, **Charles** was already married. **Henry** wanted to align England with France and betrothed **Mary** to the King of France, **Louis XII**. **Louis XII** was an old man without a male heir. **Mary** pleaded with **Henry** not to force her into marriage with **Louis**, but he insisted and his only concession was that she could marry whomever she wanted after **Louis** died. **Mary** went off to France with her attendants. To ensure **Mary's** assimilation into the French culture, **Louis** dismissed all but one attendant, 7-year-old **Anne Boleyn**. The lively **Mary** quickly made sure that her marriage was not a long one. She succeeded when **King Louis**, who had tried vainly to keep up with his young wife, died 82 days after their wedding.

Henry sent his friend, **Charles Brandon**, who was recently free of his marriage, to return **Mary** to England. **Henry** made **Charles** promise not to wed **Mary** because he was planning another diplomatic marriage for her. **Mary** found out that her brother **Henry** was not living up to his promise and begged the new King of France, **Francis I**, to allow her to marry her true love, **Charles**. She also had to convince **Charles**, because **Henry** could throw him in the Tower for disobedience. **Mary** won and she married **Charles** in Paris. **Henry** eventually forgave them and allowed them to return to London. They started a family and their granddaughter, **Lady Jane Grey**, would eventually make her mark in history. **Anne Boleyn** stayed behind to serve in the court of **Claude**, wife of **Francis I**.

Meanwhile, back in England, **Henry** and **Catherine of Aragon** still hadn't produced an heir. Finally, in 1516, **Catherine** carried a child to term, a girl they named **Mary**. In England at that time, a girl could not be heir to the throne and her main purpose was to be married off to create foreign alliances. **Henry** longed for a son, but, year after year, **Catherine** would become pregnant only to miscarry.

Henry had a few affairs and even produced a son, but he continued to hope that **Catherine** would give him the male heir he longed for; that is, until **Anne Boleyn** caught his eye upon returning from Paris. Every other women **Henry** had wanted had given into his amorous advances, but **Anne** refused. She insisted that she was saving herself for her future husband. **Henry** was smitten and she boldly spoke to him as no one else would dare. Their attraction continued for years, as **Henry** tried every avenue to rid himself of **Catherine** so he could marry **Anne**. Eventually, **Anne** gave in to **Henry's** advances and became pregnant. Convinced that this was his chance for a legitimate male heir, **Henry** broke from the Catholic Church, declaring himself King of not only England, but the head of the Church of England. By doing so, he could pronounce his marriage to **Catherine** invalid due to the fact that she had been married to his brother and thereby, made his daughter, **Mary**, illegitimate. This would make way for the son he was certain to have with **Anne Boleyn**. **Henry** and **Anne** were married. She was now **Queen Anne**. Her coronation started with 50 decorated barges floating from Greenwich to The Tower, where she spent the nights prior to her coronation at Westminster Abbey. Now **Anne** awaited the birth of the "prince." But alas, **Princess Elizabeth** was born. **Anne's** heart sank, for she knew only a son would appease her husband. **Henry** was so bewildered, he didn't attend the baptism.

Anne's family rose and fell along with **Anne**. Her brother and closest confidant, **George Boleyn**, was made **Viscount Rochford**. He was unhappily married to **Jane Parker** (now **Lady Rochford**), and the marriage was never consummated. **Jane** was a conniving, bitter woman who was jealous of **Anne's** close relationship with **George**. **Anne's** sister, **Mary Boleyn**, had once been a mistress of **Henry VIII**. **Mary** bore two children, **Henry** and **Catherine**, and it is probable that **Henry** fathered them. **Mary's** life soon changed and she married and left court for a life in the country.

Anne became pregnant again and again, only to miscarry. Her final pregnancy produced a malformed son who did not survive. Once again, **Henry** started looking for a wife that could produce a male heir and found **Jane Seymour**. She had learned well from **Anne**, telling **Henry** she was saving herself for her husband.

Anne's marriage was soon declared void and she was accused of incest with her brother **George** (this would explain why her last child was deformed) and adultery with other men. She was brought to the

Tower for trial. **George's** wife, **Lady Rochford,** testified against them, as did others. **Anne, George** and the other men were beheaded for treason. **Elizabeth, Anne** and **Henry's** daughter, was declared a bastard.

Within 24 hours of **Anne's** death, **Henry** and **Jane Seymour** were betrothed at Hampton Court. They married 9 days later. Soon **Jane** was pregnant. At last **Henry** had a boy, **Edward, Prince of England. Jane** never recovered from the birth and died twelve days later.

Henry didn't marry again for two years. This time he married for political reasons, which proved to be a disaster. While searching to combine a political alliance with sexual attraction, he commissioned an artist to draw portraits of suitable candidates. Based on a flattering portrait, he chose **Anne of Cleves.** Upon meeting her, he found that she was not attractive, and he never consummated the marriage. He quickly divorced her and declared her his "favorite" sister, avoiding disgrace to her family.

Henry was soon in love with **Katharine Howard,** a cousin of **Anne Boleyn.** She was young, beautiful and, unbeknownst to **Henry,** had a very colorful past. **Katharine** was in love with **Thomas Culpeper,** but once **Henry** became interested in her, she was persuaded by her family to marry **Henry.** Although she married **Henry,** she was able to secretly continue the affair with **Culpeper** through the help of her Lady in waiting, **Lady Rochford** (George Boleyn's wife who testified against him and his sister **Anne,** leading to their death). While praying in the Chapel at Hampton Court, **Henry** was told of **Katharine's** affair. **Katharine** tried to reach him, but was stopped by the guards in the hall. **Katharine** was taken to The Tower along with **Lady Rochford** and they were both accused and tried for treason. They were beheaded on Tower Green.

Henry's sixth and final wife was **Catherine Parr,** a wealthy widow. She was in love with **Thomas Seymour,** but he stepped aside when **Henry** fell for **Catherine.** By this time, **Henry** was an old man, obese and plagued with smelly leg ulcers. **Catherine** not only tended to his leg wounds, but the wounds of his heart. She convinced him that he should reclaim both of his daughters, **Mary** and **Elizabeth.** They were both put back into the line of succession following their brother, **Edward; Mary** first, and then, **Elizabeth.**

You may want to memorize this little rhyme that school children use to keep the fates of **Henry's** six wives straight:

Divorced, beheaded, died
Divorced, beheaded, survived.

Upon **Henry VIII's** death on January 28, 1547, **Edward**, age 9, became **King Edward VI.** One of his protectors was **John Dudley,** who realized **Edward's** fragile health. **Dudley** convinced **Edward** to name **Lady Jane** his successor. She was the granddaughter of **Mary** (**Henry's** sister) and **Charles Brandon,** which made **Jane** his second cousin, once removed. Both **Edward** and **Lady Jane** followed the English faith and she was favored over his oldest sister, **Mary,** who was a staunch Catholic. **John Dudley** had his son **Guildford** marry **Lady Jane** to ensure that his family's power would continue. **Edward VI** died at age 15; four days later **Lady Jane** was proclaimed **Queen Jane.**

Queen Jane's reign was short. Nine days later, **Mary** and her supporters rode into London, sending **Lady Jane** and the **Dudleys** to the Tower. Later, **Lady Jane,** her husband, **Guildford** and his father, **John Dudley,** were executed at the Tower.

Queen Mary I, like her mother **Catherine of Aragon,** was a Catholic. Her first act was to repeal the Protestant religion. She persecuted Protestants sending nearly 300 people to be burned at the stake for heresy, hence her nickname, **Bloody Mary. Mary** sent her half-sister, **Elizabeth,** to the Tower for allegedly conspiring against her. Seventeen years earlier, **Elizabeth's** mother, **Anne Boleyn,** had been sent to the Tower and executed. **Robert Dudley, John Dudley's** son was held at the Tower at the same time as **Elizabeth. Robert** and **Elizabeth** had been friends since childhood. They were both later released.

Queen Mary further infuriated her subjects by marrying **Phillip II** of Spain. He was not only Catholic but also a foreigner. **Phillip** was only interested in using England to finance a war with France. He spent little time with **Mary** or in England. After two phantom pregnancies, **Mary** died without an heir.

Elizabeth I, daughter of **Henry VIII** and **Anne Boleyn,** became queen of England. **Elizabeth** had inherited a country that was torn by religion, financially insecure, and at war with France. She restored Protestantism as the religion of England but gave concessions to the Catholics, easing the religious conflict. Economically, England was near ruin, but **Elizabeth** prudently handled England's finances and the country's assets became sound. She ended the war with France and later her fleet defeated the Spanish Armada. **Elizabeth** was a brilliant leader and was loved by her people.

    Elizabeth considered herself married to her kingdom and pursued the idea of her own nuptials with extreme caution, even though England needed heirs. Ultimately, she did not want to lose her power to a husband. She was also in love with men that she couldn't marry. The handsome and dashing **Robert Dudley** was first in her heart through most of her reign. They had known each other since childhood and were prisoners at the same time in the Tower. However, **Robert** also had a wife who died under mysterious circumstances. When he realized **Elizabeth** would never marry him, he married her cousin **Lettice**. **Elizabeth** felt betrayed, banishing both of them from the court. She missed **Robert** and allowed him, but not **Lettice**, back into the court. **Robert** brought **Lettice's** son, **Robert Devereux**, the **Earl of Essex**, with him. **Robert Devereux** soon replaced his stepfather as **Elizabeth's** favorite. He was rash and pompous, eventually trying to lead a revolt against **Elizabeth**. He ended up going to the Tower and losing his head. Never marrying, **Elizabeth** was known as the "Virgin Queen." Her reign spanned 40 years and is referred to as the Golden Age. At **Elizabeth's** death, **James I (James VI of Scotland)**, the son of **Mary Queen of Scots**, succeeded her.

TOWER OF LONDON

The Tower of London

The Tower of London has stood in one form or another on this spot for over 900 years. During this time it has served as a fortress, palace, and prison. Our tour of the Tower will highlight the Tudor times and touch on the people who were discussed in the recommended books.

When you enter the Tower, you have a choice to either take the Beefeaters' tour or go on your own. If you want to experience British humor at its best, the Beefeater tour is for you. Beefeaters are as colorful as their outfits, and make the tour fun with their knowledgeable replies. If you want to know where Anne Boleyn was beheaded, they may reply, "Right about here," pointing to their neck. They are also known as Yeoman Warders and guard the Tower, along with members of the British Army unit. To become a Yeoman Warder is serious business; service of twenty two years from the Royal Air Force, Royal Navy, Royal Marines, or Army is required. Also all candidates must be senior non-commissioned officers with a good record. We firmly believe a stint with Monty Python must also be part of their training. After the tour, your knowledge of Beefeaters will expand beyond the famous picture on the gin bottle.

Visitor Information
Hours: Mar. 1- Oct. 31
Tues.-Sat. 0900-1800, Sun.-Mon. 1000-1800
Nov. 1- Feb. 28
Tues.-Sat.0900-1700, Sun.-Mon. 1000-1700
Closed Jan. 1 and Dec. 24-26
Admission: Purchase tickets at the gate, on the website, or, with the British Heritage pass, admission is half price.
See Insider Tips for more information.
Underground: Tower Hill
Website: www.hrp.org.uk

The Tour

As you enter the Tower, look to your left and then up towards the hill. This is known as Tower Hill, and a scaffold once marked the spot where public executions took place. Most people were executed here, but a privileged few had a more private death within the tower walls.

Going through the main entrance to the Byward Tower, you'll cross the dry moat. The Byward Tower contains the Byward postern, one of three water entrances to the Tower. Although it is not known for sure which entrance was used, we have listed where, traditionally, it is thought people in our guide entered the Tower.

Anne Boleyn came to the Tower to await her coronation on June 1, 1533. After years of struggle, **Henry** and **Anne** had finally wed and now she would be crowned Queen. She was brought to the Tower from Greenwich by water, escorted by fifty barges richly decorated in cloths of gold. Each barge contained minstrels playing music, which was difficult to hear over the firing of celebratory artillery. The firing was so loud that there was no glass left in the windows around the Tower. She probably entered the Tower through the Byward postern. Walk straight ahead, and to your right will be Traitors' Gate. This is where tradition has it that **Anne Boleyn** returned to the Tower three years later for her execution.

It was long believed that **Anne's** daughter, **Elizabeth**, also arrived at the Tower through this gate after being accused by her half-sister, **Mary I**, of treason. More recent research has suggested that **Elizabeth** entered the Tower across the main drawbridge. She was held at the Tower for a few months before being released. When **Elizabeth** returned to the Tower before her coronation, she entered as her mother **Anne Boleyn** first had, through the Byward postern. After being crowned Queen, **Elizabeth** never returned to the Tower.

Turn around and enter into the courtyard; on your left is the Bloody Tower. This is where the two **Princes** (**Edward** and **Richard**) were believed to be held on orders from their uncle and protector, **Richard**. They disappeared and their uncle became **King Richard III**. In 1674, the bodies of two small boys were found during restorations of the White Tower. Presumed to be the bodies of the Princes, they were reburied at Westminster.

Sir Walter Raleigh was also held in the Bloody Tower during most of his thirteen years of imprisonment. He had been a favorite of **Elizabeth I**, until he had a love affair with one of her maids of honor. **Elizabeth** was jealous and sent him to the Tower for a few months; he was eventually released. **Raleigh** returned as a prisoner under **James I**, who ultimately had him beheaded.

To the right of the Bloody Tower lies Wakefield Tower. This displays replicas of torture devices used at the Tower. The three that are shown are the rack, manacles, and scavenger's daughter. Each is explained in a touch-screen display.

Head to the White Tower, begun by William the Conqueror in 1078, the oldest building within the Tower walls. The first room you will enter is the Chapel of St. John the Evangelist. This beautiful whitewashed chapel was the scene of three events in Tudor history: the mother of **Henry VIII**, **Elizabeth of York**, laid in state after her death in the Tower during childbirth, the reluctant **Lady Jane Grey** was proclaimed Queen of England, and **Mary I** became engaged to **Phillip of Spain**.

The Royal Armoury is also found on the first floor. The large case displays original armor made for **Henry VIII** when he was in his late twenties. It also contains armor for his horse. He was married to

Catherine of Aragon at this time and you can see H&K (Catherine was also spelled Katherine) on the steel skirt. The decorations also include the Tudor Rose and the pomegranate, Catherine's badge. This suit of armor was probably made for Henry's meeting with French King Francis I at the Field of Cloth of Gold.

Chapel of St. John

Next to the case is an incredibly large lance that belonged to Charles Brandon, Henry VIII's best friend and brother-in-law. Notice the portrait of Henry VIII on the wall behind the lance. This image of Henry was painted in the Holbein style, a favorite of Henry's. In the large case is another suit of armor made when Henry VIII was married to Anne Boleyn's cousin, Katharine Howard. Twenty years and four wives later, Henry's girth had certainly changed!

On the second floor is a portrait of Thomas Seymour, the brother of Henry VIII's third wife, Jane Seymour. Thomas married Henry VIII's last wife, Catherine Parr, following Henry's death. A young Elizabeth came to live with them. Thomas made advances on the young Elizabeth and she was sent to live elsewhere. He was later convicted of treason and executed.

Henry VIII armor with H&K

The Spanish Armoury is the located on the ground floor, one floor down from the main level. It contains instruments of torture, and other fearful objects such as the block that was used for the last beheading at Tower Hill in 1747. The axe that is shown is from the Tudor period.

In the Line of Kings Room, the first glass case on the right displays the heads of kings, including **Henry VIII**. The second glass case holds a green breastplate that is embellished with painted gold brocade. This once belonged to **Will Somers**, who was the fool for **Henry VIII** and his children. After exiting the White Tower, head to the Jewel House.

The Jewel House contains the Crown Jewels of England, which are magnificent. Unfortunately, the Crown Jewels, the oldest dating from the time of **Edward the Confessor** who died in 1066, were all melted down during the Interregnum (1649-1660), with the exception of the Anointing Spoon, which was used at **Henry VIII's** coronation.

After you have finished viewing the Crown Jewels, head to the Tower Green, where people of high rank were executed. It was a very exclusive club, with only seven people being executed around this site from 1483 to 1601. Those seven were:

Lord William Hastings, who was executed on orders of **Richard III**.

Queen Anne Boleyn, the second wife of Henry VIII. She was accused of adultery with five men, including her brother George. Anne was imprisoned in the identical state room that she occupied during her coronation a few years earlier. Her family was not allowed to visit her during her confinement. By eyewitness accounts, Anne walked almost gaily from the Queen's House to her execution, seemingly relieved that the event was finally at hand. Anne was the only one beheaded in the French style, with a sword while kneeling; the others met their end with the block and axe. This was a parting gift from her husband Henry. Anne had a great fear of being burned at the stake (one option of execution) and death by the axe was sometimes long and gruesome. Henry had a special sword and executioner brought over from France so the woman he once loved could have a swift and painless death.

Margaret, Countess of Salisbury was executed by order of Henry VIII, because she was the last of the Plantagenet family with rights to the crown. Legend has it that she refused to lay her head on the block, so the executioner had to chase the 68-year-old. He won.

Queen Katharine Howard, fifth wife of Henry VIII and cousin of Anne Boleyn, was accused of adultery and for coming into her marriage unchaste. She had the execution block brought to her room prior to her beheading, so she could practice laying her head on it.

Jane Parker (aka Viscountess Rochford and wife of Anne Boleyn's brother George), was Katharine's Lady of the Privy Chamber. She was accused of assisting Katharine in seeing her lover Thomas Culpeper. She had testified against both Anne and George prior to their executions. Jane's speech before her own beheading was said to have been too long, listing too many vices and drawing complaints from the onlookers.

Lady Jane Grey, wife of Guildford Dudley, was queen for nine days. The reluctant queen knelt to pray, and then insisted on putting on her own blindfold. Not being able to see, she had difficulty finding the block and a bystander had to assist her. Jane died at age 16, wanting neither the Crown nor her husband. She had been a pawn in the Dudley's search for power.

Robert Devereux, Earl of Essex, son of Lettice and stepson of Robert Dudley, was accused of plotting to overthrow Queen Elizabeth I. It has been said that he would have received a lighter sentence if he had not burst into **Queen Elizabeth's** bedroom and seen her without makeup or wig. He had been her "favorite," but seeing **Elizabeth**, as the elderly woman she was, shattered his chances for any leniency. It took three swings of the executioners' axe to complete **Robert's** beheading.

The above are all buried in St. Peter ad Vincula, just north of the Tower Green. All of the gravesites are found at the altar. Left to right, as the altar cloth touches the floor, are buried **Anne Boleyn**, **Katharine Howard**, **Jane Parker** and her husband **George Boleyn**. In front of them lie **Guildford Dudley**, **Jane Grey**, **Thomas Howard the Duke of Norfolk**, **Philip Howard the Earl of Arundel**, **Robert Devereux the Earl of Essex**, and **Thomas Overbury**. The **Countess of Salisbury** is also buried within the church.

St. Peter ad Vincula

When the crypt in the center of the church was moved in 1876, it was found to be empty, except for the baptismal font that you see by the entrance. It is decorated with the Tudor rose and may have been used as a baptismal font for the Tudor royals.

The only way to enter St. Peter ad Vincula is on the Beefeaters' Tour, with the exception of the last 45 minutes of the day, when you can enter on your own

Across the green you can see what is now called the Queen's House. At the time of **Anne Boleyn's** imprisonment, the Royal Apartments were located south of the White Tower. This is where she spent her days prior to her coronation and execution.

The Beauchamp Tower also held high-ranking prisoners; among them, the **Duke of Northumberland, John Dudley,** and his sons, **Guildford, Henry, Ambrose** and **Robert.** The **Dudleys** left several graffiti markings denoting their stay, which you can still see on the walls today. A door opposite the entrance, leads to a small room that the Yeoman Warder (Beefeater to us) told us was one of the most haunted in the Tower. After talking with him for awhile we asked if he had ever been in the room. He responded that he had, and asked us if we would like to view the haunted room which also contained more etchings. We jumped at the chance. While we were looking around the room, we heard the door shut and lock behind us. Yes, not only are the Yeomen full of information; they are also quite the jokesters!

The Bell Tower holds the curfew bell which rings each night to alert visitors of the Tower's closing. For about 500 years, the bell rang to warn of danger, signaling the guards to raise the drawbridges. **Anne Boleyn** was brought to the Bell Tower and forced to watch the executions of the five men that were accused of committing adultery with her. The Tower offers a view of the Tower Green where the men, including her brother, were beheaded. Prisoners were also held here; among them was **Sir Thomas More.** He had once been a close friend of **Henry VIII,** but when he refused to acknowledge **Henry** as the head of the Church, he was brought here and later executed. **Henry's** own daughter, **Elizabeth,** was held in the Bell Tower during her imprisonment. She was allowed to walk the battlements perhaps even as far as the Beauchamp Tower where **Robert Dudley** was held. She later returned to the Tower prior to her coronation, stating that her time at the Tower had changed her forever. She was one of the lucky ones...she lived!

The Haunted Tower

Given its gruesome history of executions, torture, hangings, and other murderous acts, it is no wonder that the Tower is said to be haunted. There are documented accounts and stories of paranormal experiences from guards, residents, and tourists.

The ghostly spirits of the two young princes, twelve-year-old

Edward V and his brother, nine-year-old **Richard, the Duke of York,** have been spied in the Bloody Tower. It is speculated that they were murdered in the Tower under the orders of their uncle **Richard III,** who inherited the throne upon their disappearance. Fifteenth century guards are said to have spotted two ghostly, child-like figures dressed in white gowns within the Bloody Tower. In 1674, the skeletal remains of two children were found under a staircase in the White Tower and are believed to be the bones of the princes. Those remains have been placed in a small marble tomb at Westminster Abbey.

Anne Boleyn has been seen on frequent occasions at different sites within the Tower. Sometimes **Anne** is carrying her decapitated head in her hands and at other times her head is still attached to her body. One night a guard captain and sentry inspected the Chapel Royal of St. Peter ad Vincula, because it was mysteriously lit. The captain stood on a tomb outside the chapel and witnessed a phantom procession of men and women dressed in Tudor apparel proceeding down the aisle in a supernatural blue and white glow. At the head of the procession was **Anne Boleyn,** who is buried beneath the altar within the church. In 1864, a guard apparently stabbed a headless apparition with his bayonet; it was believed to be **Anne,** and his blade passed right through her. He fainted and was accused of sleeping on the job, but other guards collaborated his story, claiming they had witnessed similar events. The spirit of **Anne Boleyn** has also been seen walking the Tower Green, the sight of her grisly execution.

It is said that the brutal death of the **Countess of Salisbury** is reenacted by ghostly figures on the anniversary of her death. The sixty-eight year old refused to lay her head on the block and was chased and hacked to death by the executioner.

The Salt Tower is perhaps the most ominous place within the Tower compound. Dogs are unwilling to enter the area and Beefeaters refuse to enter after dusk. A Beefeater revealed how he was nearly strangled by a powerful invisible force inside the Salt Tower. On February 12, 1957, a sentry came in contact with a ghostly figure at the Salt Tower. He heard a thud on the roof of his sentry post and when he looked, he saw an apparition upon the Tower. It was believed to be the ghost of **Lady Jane Grey,** marking the anniversary of her execution on February 12, 1554.

Lord Guildford Dudley, the husband of **Lady Jane Grey,** has been known to haunt the Beauchamp Tower. He was imprisoned there prior to his execution on Tower Hill. His ghostly presence has been seen weeping and floating within the Beauchamp Tower.

Maybe Munin?

You will probably notice the flock of ravens within the Tower walls. According to legend, the ravens must be at the Tower or both the monarchy and the Tower will fall. Not taking any chances, it was decreed under the monarchy of **Charles II** that there should always be six ravens at the Tower. These six ravens are tended by the Raven Master, who apparently has his hands full. Grog, a veteran raven of 21 years, managed to escape one day and was last spotted in 1981 at a pub called The Rose and Punchbowl. To help avoid escapes, the Raven Master clips the lifting feathers and feeds the ravens delicacies of raw meat, blood-drenched bird biscuits, a weekly egg, and as a special treat, rabbit. It is fun to note that a few ravens have been dismissed over the years for unruly behavior. After 11 years of service, Raven George was banished to the Welsh Mountain Zoo, because he has a passion for the television aerials. Two naughty birds were actually dismissed by a Tower Order, which read: "...for conduct unbecoming Tower residents, Ravens Hugine and Jackie were removed from the Tower establishment." They are probably lucky they were dismissed heads intact and weren't baked in a pie for the King! Actually, the birds can be rather endearing and the Tower wouldn't be the same without them. Raven Thor was an excellent mimic and used to mischievously imitate the Raven Master, which created all sorts of fun. One of the most popular ravens was born in 1989, and had the distinction of being the first bred raven at the Tower in over 300 years. Before that babies were brought in from various parts of England to live at the Tower. A contest was held for British schoolchildren to name the bird. Ronald Raven was the winning entry, which poked fun at the U.S. president of that time. The six ravens reside by the Wakefield Tower and include three males, Bran, Gwyllum and Cedric and three females Hugine, Branwen and Munin. Be sure to go greet them!

Now that you are in the know about the Tower history, you may find the following picture fascinating! While on the Tower tour, our friends Judy and Karen captured an interesting photo of some "maintenance workers" at the Tower. One can only speculate what they may be dragging.

Hints: Take the Beefeaters' Tour. The tour is wonderful and the only way to get into St. Peter's Chapel except for the last 45 minutes before closing, when you can enter on your own.

Buy your tickets ahead online, especially if you are also planning to go to Hampton Court. Not only will you save money, you'll save a lot of time not having to wait in line. Buy tickets at: Historic Royal Palaces www.hrp.org.uk or, if you purchase the Great British Heritage Pass (see Insider's Tips), admittance is half price. To purchase, visit www.raileurope.com go to British products and scroll down to Great British Heritage Pass.

HAMPTON COURT PALACE

Hampton Court was acquired by **Cardinal Wolsey** from the Knights Hospitallers. **Wolsey** developed it into his riverside country retreat. **Wolsey** was **Henry VIII's** second in charge and he built such a beautiful "palace" that **Henry** became jealous of it. When **Wolsey** failed to obtain **Henry's** divorce from **Catherine of Aragon** and began to fall out of favor, he wisely offered Hampton Court to **Henry** as a show of his loyalty. King William III and Queen Mary II rebuilt the Palace in the 1690's. While it still retains much of the Tudor history, it includes both original architecture and reproductions of the Tudor times.

Hampton Court Palace

Visitor Information

Hours: Late Mar.-late Oct.
Tues.-Sun. 0930-1800 Mon. 1015-1800
Late Oct.-late Mar.
Tues.-Sun. 0930-1630 Mon. 1015-1630
Admission: Purchase tickets at the gate, on the website, or, with the British Heritage pass, admission is free. See Insider Tips for more information.
Location: East Molesey
Website: www.hrp.org.uk
How to get there: For a direct route with no changes, go to Waterloo Station and take the Southwest Train to Hampton Court. The trains run at 26 and 56 minutes after the hour. The trip takes about 30 minutes. Hampton court is a short walk from the station, just over the bridge. If you have a Travelcard that includes Zone 6, there is no charge. Also, there is no need to exchange the card for a train ticket

The Tour

After acquiring the palace, **Henry VIII** rebuilt Hampton Court, putting his mark on what became one of the most impressive palaces in England. As you walk across the moat bridge to the main entrance, notice the lion statues that line the bridge. They carry the badges of **Henry VIII** and his third wife, **Jane Seymour**. Above the gateway are the arms of **Henry VIII**. Pass through the gateway into the first courtyard, Base Court. This court looks much the same as it did in **Henry's** time. If you look back over the gateway, you can see another carving of **Henry's** coat of arms.

On both sides are turrets containing the initials E R (**Elizabeth Regina**) and badges of his daughter, **Elizabeth**. Walk through the court to the **Anne Boleyn** Gateway. Underneath the gate, stop and look up to see the carved letters H and A. This stands for **Henry VIII** and **Anne Boleyn,** one of the few remaining references to their marriage.

As you pass through the gate, you will enter the Clock Court. Look back over the **Anne Boleyn** Gateway at the clock from which this court was named. **Henry** commissioned this clock during his marriage to **Katharine Howard**. At the time this Astronomical Clock was built it was thought that the sun revolved around the earth. Below the clock is evidence of the previous owner, **Cardinal Wolsey**. Angels display **Wolsey's** coat of arms and the **Cardinal's** hat in a terra cotta design (these arms were put back in the Victorian period). Opposite the clock were the former Tudor Royal Apartments. The upper rooms were used by **Catherine of Aragon**, the middle suite by **Henry**, and the ground floor rooms by their daughter **Mary**. Unfortunately, they were later rebuilt.

The Astronomical Clock

The seventeenth century Colonnade to the right, hides the rooms that were used by **Cardinal Wolsey** and later by **Henry VIII's** sixth wife, **Catherine Parr**. Return to the **Anne Boleyn** Gateway and proceed up the stairway to the Tudor State Apartments. On the left is a room where you can view an introductory video. The doorway has the Tudor Rose on one side and the pomegranates of **Catherine of Aragon** on the other. This area had not been built during their marriage, so this door was relocated during a restoration.

Enter the Great Hall. In the ceiling are the coats of arms of **Anne Boleyn** and **Henry VIII**. In the wooden screen above the entrance door are the initials of **Henry** and **Anne**. The H and A are intertwined to show their love. The gaps in the screen show where some of their initials were hastily removed to prepare for the wedding of **Henry** to **Jane Seymour**.

The stained glass window, made during Victorian time, shows **Henry** and all of his wives' coats of arms.

The tapestries are of Abraham, who trusts in God's promise that he will give him a son to succeed him. **Henry** commissioned this work when he was married to **Anne Boleyn**. During the reign of **King James I**, the Great Hall was the location of many festivities. These included plays that were performed and written by **William Shakespeare**.

The Horn Room is next. This was a waiting area for servants of the Great Hall and the Great Watching Chamber. The Great Watching Chamber is where the Yeomen of the Guard protected the entrance to the King's private rooms. It is also where important officials would dine. The ceiling contains the badges of **Henry** and **Jane Seymour**. The tapestries are all from the collection of **Thomas Wolsey**, depicting the story of the conflict between Virtues and Vices. Three of the small tapestries above the door show the arms of **Cardinal Wolsey**; the other shows the arms of **Henry**. The declarations regarding **Queen Katharine Howard's** extramarital affairs were publicly announced in this room. Immediately following the declarations, **Katharine** and her household were dismissed.

The Processional Gallery connects the Great Watching Gallery to the Haunted Gallery. Off the Processional Gallery is the Page's Chambers, where pages would wait to serve the nobles. Courtiers also used this room to change into their ceremonial robes before seeing the King. There is a portrait of **Henry VIII** over the fireplace.

Back in the processional Gallery is a portrait of **Edward VI** as a young boy, emulating the pose of his father and dressed in rich clothing, looking every bit a future king. What is fascinating about this area is that the woodwork around the windows contains hundreds of years of graffiti. A guard told us that the outline of **Anne Boleyn's** hand is here. Although we really don't believe this, it is fun to find. It has been said, but never proven, that **Anne** had an extra fingernail or part of a finger on her right hand and wore long sleeves to cover the deformity. The song Greensleeves is attributed to **Henry VIII** and it is said that he wrote the song for **Anne**. There are also rumors that **Anne** had a third breast, which was possibly a vestigial nipple, and also a strawberry mole located on her neck. Her enemies claimed these were all signs of a witch.

The Haunted Gallery contains many pieces of art that pertain to **Henry VIII** and his family. The first painting you encounter is a portrait of **Henry VIII** painted in the Holbein style, a style favored by **Henry**.

The Embarkation of **Henry VIII** from Dover shows **Henry** on his flagship with the golden sails, The Great Harry.

The family portrait shows **Henry** in the middle with his son and heir, **Edward**, on his right. On **Edward's** right is **Mary**, next in line to the throne. To the left of **Henry** is **Jane**, and standing in the distance to **Jane's** left is **Elizabeth** .The man with the monkey is **Will Somers**, the fool of **Henry VIII**. It is a wonderful family portrait, though **Jane** had died when **Edward** was an infant and she never saw her son at this age.

The painting of the Field of Cloth of Gold shows the meeting of **Henry VIII** and **King Francis I** of France.

The last painting shows **Henry VII** and his wife **Elizabeth of York** and **Henry VIII** and his wife **Jane Seymour**. This was obviously painted after his parents' death.

The Haunted Gallery is named from the reported presence of **Queen Katharine Howard's** ghost. **Katharine** was trying vainly to reach her husband and beg his forgiveness after he had found out about her affair. The guards stopped her in the Gallery, preventing her from reaching **Henry** who was in the Royal Pews. According to legend, **Katharine's** ghost still runs screaming down this hallway, pleading for **Henry** to forgive her.

During the reign of **Henry VIII**, the Royal Pew was divided into two rooms, one for the king and one for the queen. It was in the queen's chamber that **Henry** was married to his last wife **Catherine Parr**.

The ceiling in the Chapel proper is magnificently carved and gilded. **Henry** had it installed after he acquired Hampton Court. During **Henry's** reign, there was a large stained glass window at the far end of the chapel. It is now hidden by a large oak screen. As you leave the chapel, you can see the arms of **Henry** and **Jane Seymour** flanking the outside of the door.

Henry's daughter **Mary** chose Hampton Court as the site of her honeymoon with her ill-suited husband, **Phillip of Spain**. **Elizabeth**, while queen, chose Hampton Court with all of its splendor, to impress dignitaries. Neither **Mary** nor **Elizabeth** made many changes to the Palace during their reigns; **Henry** had left the Palace magnificent.

The grounds around Hampton Court are stunning at any time of the year. It contains ornamental gardens, statues and tree lined paths. We came upon, by all appearances, a small garden maze in which we became hopelessly lost. Actually the maze consists of winding pathways that stretch about a half a mile, and have very tall hedges that define its path. It is fun, challenging, and will have you moving in all sorts of directions. Luckily for us we were led to safety by a group of visiting school children. Be sure to roam the gardens on your visit, but enter the maze with either a group of children or leave bread crumbs to find your way out!

Haunted Hampton Court

Several ghosts from the Tudor period have been sighted at Hampton Court. **Cardinal Wolsey** probably still considers Hampton his home, since his spirit has been seen at his old apartments.

Possibly the most famous apparition is of **Katharine Howard**, who has been sighted in a white gown, floating down the Haunted Gallery. On several occasions, **Anne Boleyn** has been spotted wandering the corridors, apparently looking appalled by her ill fate.

Jane Seymour is said to be **Henry VIII's** favorite wife, since she gave birth to his only male heir, **Edward VI**. Unfortunately, **Jane** died at Hampton Court shortly after **Edward** was born. Witnesses have seen **Jane's** spirit walking in Clock Court holding a lit candle and wearing a white gown.

Sibell Penn was **Prince Edward VI's** nurse and cared for him after **Jane's** death. **Sibell** died of smallpox and was buried on the grounds at Hampton Court. In 1829, workmen disturbed her remains and soon after, strange whirling sounds were detected in an area located in the southwest wing of Hampton Court. The sound was traced to a small, concealed room behind a brick wall; the room contained a spinning wheel similar to the one that **Sibell** used. **Sibell** has been seen and heard around the castle on several occasions. In 1986 her apparition, dressed in gray, was noticed wandering the enclosed corridors and courtyards of Hampton Court.

On October 7, 2003, a security camera caught the most extraordinary ghost opening and closing a fire door at apartment 35 at Hampton Court. The ghost was dressed in period costume and a security guard described its face as not looking human. There are guides at Hampton that dress in period costume, but this costume does not appear in their collection. The actual security camera footage can be viewed on line on several websites, including www.hrp.org.uk (type in Hampton Court ghost in their search engine). During your visit, be sure to check out apartment 35!

WINDSOR CASTLE

Windsor Castle

Windsor Castle is one of the official residences of the **Queen Elizabeth II** and it is said to be her favorite. When the Royal Standard is flying high above the Round Tower of Windsor Castle, the queen is in attendance. If the Union Jack flag is spotted, she is elsewhere. Windsor Castle was first built in 1066 and overlooks the River Thames. It is the largest occupied castle in the world and the structure stretches over 12 acres. On November 20, 1992, a devastating fire swept through the castle and damaged over 100 rooms. Fortunately, the rooms were in the midst of being renovated; most of the valuable pieces were not harmed since they were stored elsewhere. Ironically, the fire took place on the forty-fifth wedding anniversary of **Queen Elizabeth II** and the **Duke of Edinburgh**. After £37 million in extensive renovations, the castle was reopened to the public in 1997.

Windsor Castle has existed over 900 years and has been altered by several of the monarchies. Members of the Tudor dynasty have added their own special touches to Windsor. In the Upper Ward, **Henry VII** built his own personal apartments and **Elizabeth I** enhanced them by adding the Long Gallery, which is presently the Royal Library. The North Terrace, which was also built by **Elizabeth I**, overlooks the Thames and Eton. **Elizabeth I** enjoyed her daily exercise and would either walk the Gallery or The North Terrace, depending on the weather. **Elizabeth I** also hunted on the grounds and liked archery. Her love of the dramatic arts led her to build a stage inside the castle. Allegedly, **Shakespeare** wrote the play, "The Merry Wives of Windsor" at the request of **Elizabeth**, and some sources say it was performed for her at Windsor. In the Lower Ward, **Mary** oversaw the construction of the Military Knights' Houses. **Henry VII** and **Henry VIII** both contributed to St. Georges Chapel. **Henry VIII**, of course, built the great entrance in the Lower Ward, referred to as **Henry VIII Gate**. It is well documented that his son, **Edward VI**, disliked staying at Windsor and, coincidently, added nothing to its structure. **King Charles II** completely refurbished the State Apartments into the Baroque style during his reign; therefore little remains from the Tudor dynasty.

Windsor is a quaint town filled with wonderful shops and restaurants. You should plan on spending extra time to explore the town.

Visitor Information
Hours: Apr.-June 1000-1700
July-Aug. M-F 1000-1750, Sat. 1000-1730, Sun. 1000-1700
Sept. M-Sat. 1000-1700, Sun. 1000-1600
Oct.-Mar. M-F 1000-1600, Sat. 1000-1700, Sun. 1000-1600
Closed: Dec. 24-26, Jan.1
The State Apartments are sometimes closed for official functions, but the other sites are open. Check in advance before your visit.

St. George's Chapel

Please Note: Open every day except Sun.

Closes at 1300 on July 13, Sep. 4, and Dec. 23; closed Dec. 24-25

Changing of the Guard 1100 on alternate days, weather permitting.

Admission: Purchase tickets at the gate; with the British Heritage pass, admission is free.

See Insider Tips for more information.

How to get there: Train: From London, catch the train from the Waterloo or Paddington station. If you purchased the all-zone Travelcard, the train fare is not included. You must purchase an add-on ticket to take you from zone 6 to Windsor. You will need to change trains at Slough to get to Windsor from Paddington station. The add-on cost is £3.50 after 0930 and £6.40 before 0930. You may also purchase an individual train ticket if you don't have the zone 6 Travelcard.

Website: Visit www.royal.gov.uk for further information.

The Tour

The State Apartments

We are only listing State Apartments that contain Tudor references. The palace contains many beautiful apartments that hold collections from other monarchs.

The King's Drawing Room

This room holds a Rubens' painting of **Phillip II of Spain** dressed in an equestrian outfit. **Queen Mary I** wed the much younger **Phillip** in 1554. She was very smitten by a portrait that he had sent to her and she longed for their nuptials. On the other hand, **Phillip** married her for political purposes. Soon after their marriage, **Mary** chose Windsor as the place to hold her court.

The Queen's Drawing Room

The Tudor dynasty is well represented by portraits of **Henry VIII** and his three children: **Edward VI, Queen Mary I,** and **Queen Elizabeth I.**

The Queen's Audience Chamber

A portrait of **Mary Queen of Scots** is seen above the exit.

The Queen's Guard Chamber

This room contains a hunting sword used by **Henry VIII**.

St. George's Hall

At the far end of the room, in the music loft, is a figure mounted on a horse, a tribute to the King's Champion. The Champion would enter the coronation banquet completely armed and would then cast down his gauntlet to challenge anyone who would deny the new monarch as the rightful ruler. The Champion at the coronations of **Edward VI**, **Mary** and **Elizabeth I** was Sir Edward Dymoke, who inherited the role from his father. The gesture was an act of pageantry, since the coronation had already taken place. **King George IV** was the last ruler to use this ceremony at his coronation in 1821.

Lantern Lobby

The lobby contains a massive suit of armor worn by **Henry VIII**, one of the last made for him. While the palace was under restoration in 1992, a fabric curtain caught fire in the Lantern Lobby, causing extensive damage. A plaque symbolizes where the fire began.

The Gallery

The Gallery rotates its collection of prints, drawings, watercolors, documents and other valuable treasures. The Royal Collection holds works from master artists such as Michelangelo, Raphael and DaVinci. The exhibits are not to be missed!

Queen Mary's Dolls' House

Although, this does not follow any of the books, it is interesting to view. **Queen Mary's** (wife of **King George V**) Dolls' House is located next to the entrance of the State Apartments. Even Barbie would be jealous of this dream house! The Dolls' House is a replica of an English country manor and its contents are all one-twelfth their original size. Electric lights, running water, marble staircases, a stocked wine cellar, and functional elevators are some of the fine details that make this house so grand. The crown jewels are also secured in the Strong Room and elegant crystal and silver pieces adorn the dining area. The idea for the creation of the Dolls' House came from the suggestion of Princess Mary Louise, who noticed that **Queen Mary,** an avid collector of miniatures, was displaying them in a small doll house. The Princess contacted architect Sir Edwin Lutyens to design a magnificent house as a gift and tribute to **Queen Mary.** It was completed in 1924, after three years of construction and with the help of 1500 people.

St. George's Chapel

The Chapel is a magnificent example of late European Medieval architecture. It was constructed during the reign of **King Edward IV** and was finished approximately fifty years later when **Henry VIII** was king of England. **Henry VIII** left his mark throughout the chapel, embellishing it with the Tudor Rose and his coat of arms. **Henry** redesigned the outside of the structure by adding seventy-six stone creatures to the roof. They are known as The Windsor Royal Beasts, whose decorative function is to display coats of arms and weather vanes. There are fourteen of these heraldic animals, each holding green staffs with golden flags that refer to both the Tudor and Plantagenet Royal descendants. The Heraldic Panther of **Queen Jane Seymour** is the fifth one from the right. During the Field of the Cloth of Gold, **Henry VIII** decorated his pavilion with the beasts; subsequently, they became a favorite adornment and occupy both Windsor and Hampton Court. St. Georges Chapel is also the burial site of ten English sovereigns: **Henry VI, Edward IV, Charles I, George III, George IV, William IV, Edward VII, George V, George VI,** and **Henry VIII.** Once inside the chapel, notice the beautiful coat of arms of **Henry VIII** in the center of the ceiling.

The **George VI** Memorial Chapel contains the tomb of **King George VI,** father of **Queen Elizabeth II.** In 2002, both the **Queen Mother** and her daughter, **Princess Margaret,** were buried within the chapel. (We find it interesting that **Princess Margaret's** grave remains unmarked.)

Henry VIII is buried within the choir enclosure. Once down the aisle, notice the simple metal plate that marks the grave of **King Henry VIII.** Before his death, **Henry** envisioned that he would be memorialized with a grand effigy honoring himself and his third wife, **Jane Seymour** (his only wife to produce a male heir), in the choir area of St. George's Chapel.

This obviously did not happen. Apparently, a monument for **Henry** had been started, but during the Civil War, Parliamentarian forces occupied Windsor Castle. The memorial was damaged and its parts stolen.

There are two interesting incidents that happened after the death of **Henry VIII**. His body was taken to Windsor for burial next to his third wife, **Jane Seymour**. While on the way, his coffin was taken to Syon, which, prior to **Henry VIII's** church reformation, had been an Abbey. During the night, **Henry's** coffin burst open and body fluid from **Henry's** corpse leaked onto the church floor. In the morning, dogs were found licking up his blood. Some thought that this was a divine judgment for **Henry's** action of dissolving the Abbey in 1539. Most people were also aware of the prediction made by Friar Peto, who had stated in 1532, that if **Henry** divorced **Katherine of Aragon** to marry **Anne Boleyn**, he would be like Ahab, his blood licked up by dogs. The second incident occurred in 1813, when workers, building a passageway for the vault that would later contain **George III**, accidentally broke through the vault of **Henry VIII** and found three coffins. The first was a large, damaged coffin that contained **Henry VIII**. His casket was open and exposed his skeleton, which apparently still had some auburn strands of hair on its skull and remnants of a beard. His skeleton measured 6 feet 2 inches. Beside him was **Jane Seymour's** coffin, intact and undisturbed. Both coffins were unmarked.

King Charles I was inscribed on the third coffin. The coffin was examined and it was determined to be his remains. He had been beheaded during the English Civil War and his burial sight had been a mystery.

If you look to the left of the altar you will notice a wooden balcony. **Henry** designed the balcony for his first wife, **Catherine of Aragon**, so she could view the Garter ceremony. It is decorated with the coats of arms of both **Henry** and **Catherine**, along with the Tudor rose and her symbol, the pomegranate.

As you enter the south choir aisle, you'll notice an enclosed case in the middle of the hall. It contains a book of diagrams showing the location and dimensions of the coffins of **Henry VIII**, **Jane Seymour**, and **Charles I**. This hallway also contains a stained glass window portraying **Henry VIII**, **Jane Seymour**, **Edward VI**, and **Elizabeth I**.

Albert Memorial Chapel

King Henry VII tore down the thirteenth-century chapel that was once built on this site and started building a new chapel, intending to use it as his own mausoleum. However, he later changed his mind and commissioned the Lady Chapel at Westminster, where he is buried. **Henry VIII** gave the unfinished chapel to **Cardinal Wolsey** and it was known as **Wolsey's** Tomb House for a long time. The cardinal had a beautiful, but partially-finished, shrine in the chapel. For a while, **Henry VIII** claimed the shrine as his own. Years later, the remains of the shrine were sent to St. Paul's for Lord Nelson's use.

As you leave the castle through the Lower Ward, you will pass through the **Henry VIII Gateway**, built in 1509, during the first year of his reign. Once you are past the gate, look back over the arch to view the King's arms and the Tudor rose. Note the pomegranate, representing his first wife, **Catherine of Aragon**.

Other Interesting Historical Facts

- **Anne Boleyn** received the title Marquees of Pembroke at Windsor. **Henry** was still married to his first wife, **Catherine of Aragon**, but needed to pacify his mistress. **Anne** was in her glory, dressed in a crimson gown with her hair flowing down her shoulders.
- **Prince Charles** proposed to **Princess Diana** in the nursery at Windsor Castle.
- **Sophie Rhys-Jones** married **Prince Edward** at St. George's Chapel on June 19, 1999. Prince Edward is the youngest son of **Queen Elizabeth II**.
- On April 9, 2005, **Prince Charles** married his longtime companion, **Camilla Parker Bowles**, in a civil ceremony in Windsor's Guildhall. After the ceremony the couple proceeded to Windsor Castle for a blessing of their marriage in St. George's Chapel.

Haunted Windsor

Royal ghosts have been spotted on the premises throughout the years, so keep this in mind while you visit the grounds! Guards have witnessed a figure resembling **Henry VIII** walking near the battlements and then fading into a wall. During the reign of **Henry**, this wall was actually a doorway. The large ghostly figure was walking with a limp, which coincides with the ulcerated leg that plagued the king in his later years. The ghost of **Henry VIII** has also been seen roaming through the corridors; castle visitors have heard his moans as well as his footsteps. **Henry's** second wife, **Anne Boleyn**, has been observed several times, always wearing the same garment, a dress covered with a black lace shawl. Her ghostly figure has been seen standing at the window at Dean's Cloister; on occasion, the ghost appears to be her daughter, **Queen Elizabeth I**, peering out the window. **Anne** has been spotted in the Royal Library, and her footsteps have also been heard. Her daughter seems to have the same haunts as her mother, since she has also been spotted in the library. **Queen Elizabeth I** once appeared before Lieutenant Glynn of the Grenadier Guards, who, at the time, had his nose buried in a book within the library. Initially he heard the clicking of her high heels, and then the Queen came into focus, passing so close he could have touched her. He followed her into a room that had no other exit, but she suddenly disappeared.

The spirit of **King Charles I** has been seen in the library and it is said he also haunts the Canons House. Even though he was beheaded during the turbulent English Revolution, he has been spied with his total body intact, closely resembling his painted portraits

Apparitions of crazy **King George III** have appeared in the window of the apartment where he was once confined while being treated for mental illness. He has been heard mumbling in the vacant library, "What? What? What?" Many spirits also roam the Long Walk. A soldier ultimately committed suicide after claiming he saw the marble statues move on their own in the park. Of course, Windsor is frequented by thousands of visitors who never have a paranormal experience, but you may be one of the lucky ones!

WESTMINSTER ABBEY

Westminster Abbey

Westminster Abbey is a magnificent Gothic-style working church that is designed in the shape of a cross. The Abbey pays homage to many kings and queens of England as well as several famous Britons that are linked to its remarkable history. Between 1042 and 1065, Edward the Confessor built a church on the site of Westminster Abbey and is considered its founder.

The Tudor dynasty had a profound effect on the history of Westminster Abbey. **Henry VII** created the magnificent Lady Chapel in the east wing. When **Henry VIII** broke from the Roman Catholic Church and proclaimed himself head of the Church of England, he enacted the Dissolution of the Monasteries, which gave him the power to seize valuables and property from all the Roman Catholic Churches throughout England. Westminster's treasury was one of the first on his list and it was seized in 1534. In 1540, **Henry** disbanded the Benedictine Abbey and turned it into a cathedral. The well-known expression "robbing Peter to pay Paul" likely came from this period in history. The money intended for the Abbey, which was dedicated to St. Peter, was transferred to the coffers of St. Paul's Cathedral. When **Queen Mary I**, a Catholic, came into power, she reinstated the monks at the Abbey. During the reign of her sister, **Queen Elizabeth I**, the monks were once again evicted!

Seventeen sovereigns are buried within the Abbey; the most notable are **Queen Elizabeth I, Mary I, Mary, Queen of Scots, King Henry VII** and **King Edward VI**. With over 3,300 people buried inside the Abbey and Cloisters, the church is practically a who's who of well-known British figures, including **Charles Dickens, Sir Isaac Newton,** and **Lewis Carroll**.

Royal ceremonies continue to be held at Westminster Abbey. In 1947, **Queen Elizabeth II** and **Prince Philip** were married at Westminster. In 1997, the emotional funeral of **Princess Diana** took place at Westminster. It included a poignant eulogy from her brother, the Earl of Spencer, and a special rendition of Candle in the Wind by Elton John.

Visitor Information

Hours: Open year round
Mon.-Fri. 0930-1545
Wed. 0930-1900
Sat. 0930-1345
*Sun. Worship only – no tourist visits
Admission: Charge
Underground: St. James Park or Westminster
Website: www.westminster-abbey.org

The Tour

Begin your tour by entering the Great North Door. Move to the Lady Chapel. Keep to your left and enter the burial site of both **Queen Elizabeth I** and her half-sister, **Queen Mary I**, daughters of **Henry VIII**. It is ironic that both sisters are buried together since there was no love lost between the two. **Mary**, a Catholic, never really trusted **Elizabeth**, a Protestant, and even had her held in the Tower on the suspicion of treason. **Elizabeth's** mother, **Anne Boleyn**, had been beheaded at the Tower, which made **Elizabeth's** imprisonment unbearable. However, **Elizabeth** seems to have had the last laugh, since a magnificent marble effigy honors this queen, while "**Bloody Mary**" is buried beneath her sister and her grand memorial. The Latin phrase on the black plaques on the front of the tomb reads, "Partners both in throne and grave, here rest we two sisters, **Elizabeth** and **Mary**, in the hope of one resurrection." The far wall is called Innocent's Corner. The small, white marble tomb contains the skeletal remains of two young children, believed to be the princes **Edward V** and **Richard, Duke of York**. Their protector and uncle, **Richard, Duke of Gloucester**, brought the children to the Tower in 1483 and they were never seen again. Remains assumed to be the princes were discovered under a staircase in the Tower about 200 years later, during the reign of **Charles II**. He had their remains moved to this site at that time.

You may think only ladies are buried in the Lady Chapel, but it is also referred to as **Henry VII's** Chapel. **Henry VII** lies with his wife, **Elizabeth of York**, in the eastern end of the chapel, behind the altar. He originally started to build the chapel in 1503 as a resting spot for **Henry VI**, but **Henry VI** remains at Windsor, marked by a plain gray slab, while **Henry VII** is glorified here. Isn't it funny how things work out?

The grave of **Edward VI**, son of **Henry VIII** and **Jane Seymour**, lies under the altar at the head of the tomb of his grandfather, **Henry VII**.

While researching this book we were helped greatly by a warden on duty in this room. He directed us to Westminster's private library for assistance with our research. When we came back to thank him, he was explaining to other visitors the significance of the stalls that line the room. They are for the Order of the Bath, which is the third highest order of British chivalry. The Queen is Sovereign of the Order and her stall is the one with the canopy that sits to the left of the doorway. Once he had finished his explanation, we thanked him for his help. He replied that he thought that there should be a little "icing on the cake" and asked if we would like to sit in the Queen's stall. We followed him up to the stall and sat there while he explained the meaning behind the plaques that line the stall. After he was done talking, he asked if we had a camera, and turning to the rest of the visitors, he stated that there was no photography allowed, then turned to us and said, "say cheese!" For a moment in time we both felt like true queens, sitting in the same spot where **Henry VIII** and **Queen Elizabeth I** once sat.

The Queen's stall in Lady's Chapel

Mary Queen of Scots was a thorn throughout the reign of **Queen Elizabeth I** and lies directly across the aisle from her. Forced to abdicate her Scottish throne in favor of her infant son, **James, Mary** fled Scotland and went to England for refuge. **Queen Elizabeth** didn't quite know what to do with her and had her confined for nineteen years. **Mary** had a claim to the throne of England and was allegedly involved in a number of plots against her cousin. **Mary** was beheaded at Fotheringhay Castle for apparently scheming to kill **Queen Elizabeth**, even though she professed her innocence. **Mary** was originally buried in Peterborough Cathedral on **Elizabeth's** command, but **King James I, Mary's** son, moved her remains to Westminster in 1612 and had the white marble effigy made in her honor. **James I** was also responsible for **Elizabeth I** tomb design.

Note that **Mary's** tomb is slightly higher than **Elizabeth's**, bringing her closer to God.

As you leave the chapel, walk straight ahead to view the coronation chair. The chair was made in the reign in **Edward I**, and every ruler used it since **Edward II**, with the exception of **Edward V, Edward VIII**, and **Lady Jane Grey**, who were never crowned. **Queen Mary I**, a Catholic, refused to sit in the coronation chair when she was crowned since her Protestant half-brother **Edward** had used it and was, in her eyes, a heretic. Instead, she used a special chair blessed by the Pope for her crowning and the coronation chair became her throne. **Henry VIII** and his first wife, **Catherine of Aragon**, were both crowned together in a jubilant ceremony at Westminster Abbey on June 24, 1509. **Henry's** second wife, **Anne Boleyn**, was also crowned at Westminster, but it was a less triumphant affair. **Anne** was met with jeers as she passed by in a magnificent procession from the Tower to Westminster. Those who still favored **Catherine of Aragon** shouted, "HA! HA!," sarcastically referring to the initials of the new king and queen.

Continue down the corridor until you reach Poets' corner. This site honors prominent British poets, writers, musicians, and actors. Some are buried here and others are recognized with a memorial, but buried elsewhere. It is ironic that **Henry VIII** is indirectly responsible for the numerous burials throughout the Abbey. After **Henry** closed the monastery in 1540, the Abbey was in financial straits and needed money. The Abbey became a burial place in exchange for money. Until the nineteenth century, the wealthy were able to purchase a burial spot within the Abbey, so those buried within the Abbey aren't necessarily the most honored and distinguished people in British history, just the wealthiest for their time. Today, the Dean of Westminster supervises all burials (ashes only) and monuments within the Abbey. **Charles Dickens** is among the honored authors buried within Poets' Corner. Every June 9, on the anniversary of his death, a wreath is placed on **Dickens'** memorial. **Jane Austen** is marked with a memorial, but she is actually buried in Winchester Cathedral. Probably one of the most famous people honored is **William Shakespeare**. He was belatedly recognized with a memorial in 1740, more than one hundred years after his death. He was buried in Stratford-upon-Avon in the year 1616

Once you leave the Poets' Corner, continue to the Chapter House.

This exquisite octagonal area was once used by the Benedictine monks to conduct their daily business. Additionally, the Chapter House was where Parliament met between the reigns of **Edward I** and **Henry VIII** before transferring across the road to the palace of Westminster. Readers of *The Da Vinci Code* might imagine the confrontation between **Robert Langdon**, **Sophie** and **Teabring** that took place in the Chapter House.

Turn left outside the Chapter House hallway and continue until you come to the museum. This beautiful vaulted room was known as the undercroft and was possibly used by the monks as their common area. The museum holds a number of funeral effigies that pertain to the sovereigns and the nobility that are buried within the Abbey. The earliest effigies are made of wood and the latter are of wax. Wax likenesses were preferred in lying-in-state royal funerals, since the corpses tended to stink. The plaster head of **Queen Mary I** is at the exhibit as well as the original wooden body effigy (complete with undergarments) of her half-sister, **Queen Elizabeth I**.

Nearby is a wax effigy of **Queen Elizabeth I** that was re-made in 1760, from her monument in the Lady Chapel, the original one was made of wood. Notice the Essex ring that **Queen Elizabeth I** gave to **Robert Devereux, Earl of Essex**. The queen was infatuated with the much younger Earl and gave him the ring, with the pledge that if he ever returned it to her, it would convey forgiveness. The Earl led an ill-fated coup against the queen and was subsequently sent to the Tower for execution. Allegedly, while the Earl was imprisoned, he gave the ring to a boy with instructions to give it to Lady Scrope and then plead with her to give the ring to the queen. Unfortunately, the boy gave the ring to Scrope's sister, Lady Nottingham, whose husband was an enemy of the Earl. Lady Nottingham kept the ring and the Earl was executed. Lady Nottingham made a deathbed confession two years later to the queen about the ring incident. The queen was not amused and supposedly gave the dying Lady this terse reply, "God may forgive you madam, but I never can!"

Other jewelry includes duplicates of the Crown Jewels that are used for coronation rehearsals. The real Crown Jewels are at the Tower, so don't miss those.

Once out of the museum, head toward the nave. **Sir Isaac Newton's** monument is situated against the screen for the choir. **Newton** is probably best known for his scientific discovery of the force of gravity, which legend states came to him while he watched an apple fall from a tree. The statue and the quest for the missing orb will be especially intriguing to the readers of *The Da Vinci Code.* During one of our visits the sunlight shown through the stained glass windows, making colorful balls of light appear to dance on **Newton's** monument. If your visit is on a sunny day, look around the nave for the dancing lights; you'll never forget the experience. Exit the Abbey in the Nave. The bookshop is located outside and around the corner to your left; you'll need your ticket to enter.

NATIONAL PORTRAIT GALLERY

The National Portrait Gallery was established in 1856 with the premise that the main focus of the gallery would be history, and not art. The gallery covers a large scope of artwork, from medieval times to the present. The Tudor monarchy is well represented with portraits of significant individuals that shaped the Tudor era. You may want to review The Tudor History in the beginning of our book.

There are two full rooms of Tudor paintings as well as a third room with miniatures (Rooms 1-3). Each portrait has a detailed description, explaining the person's relevance to Tudor times. Take the time to examine all of the portraits; you will need at least an hour to fully appreciate them. They will help remind you that these were real people and not just characters in a book. We highly recommend that you visit this gallery.

Don't miss viewing the portraits of the present Royal family in room 33. Included is a portrait of **Princess Diana** that was commissioned at the time of her engagement to **Prince Charles**.

If you are hungry before or after your visit, we strongly suggest Cafe-in-the-Crypt, which is directly across the street in the basement of the church of St. Martin-in-the-Fields.

Visitor Information

Hours: Open daily 1000-1800
Late opening Thurs. and Fri. until 2100
Closed: Jan. 1, Good Friday, Dec. 24-26
Admission: Free, except for some special exhibitions.
Location: The National Portrait Gallery is on the north side of Trafalgar Square, opposite the Church of St Martin-in-the Fields.
Underground: Leicester Square or Charing Cross
Website: www.npg.org.uk

THE NATIONAL GALLERY

The National Gallery contains over 2,300 examples of Western European paintings dating from 1250 to 1900. This vast collection includes a portrait of **Christina of Denmark**, the spunky princess who had a few choice words for **Henry VIII**. It also possesses **Da Vinci's**, The Virgin of the Rocks, which is a "sister painting" of the famous Madonna of the Rocks, and is linked to *The Da Vinci Code*. Although the gallery does not contain a lot of references to our book selections, it features several superb Impressionist works that will take your breath away. The gallery also contains works from masters such as Rembrandt and Botticelli. The National Gallery is located close to the National Portrait Gallery and we recommend that you visit both!

The National Gallery

Hours: Daily 1000-1800

Wed. until 2100

Closed: Jan.1, Dec. 24-26

Admission: Free

Location: Trafalgar Square

Underground: Charing Cross and Leicester Square

Website: www.nationalgallery.org.uk/

The Tour
Christina of Denmark, Duchess of Milan
By Holbein the Younger (1538)
Room 4

Henry VIII was shopping for a new bride after the death of **Jane Seymour.** He was interested in marrying the Danish princess and arranged for Holbein to paint her portrait so he could get a good look at his prospective bride. **Christina** was sixteen years of age and a recent widow. Holbein's portrait captures her wholesome complexion which is illuminated by her dark mourning gown. This painting is truly exquisite and **Henry** was said to have been smitten with this image of **Christina.** Although youthful in appearance, she was very wise for her age. It is said that she made this response to **Henry's** proposal, "If she had two heads she would gladly put one at the King of England's disposal." She went on to marry Francois Duc de Bar and **Henry** married **Anne of Cleaves.**

The Virgin of the Rocks
By Leonardo Da Vinci (about 1492-1508)
Room 2

Da Vinci was hired to paint the central panel of a triptych for the altar of the church of San Francesco Grande, by the organization referred to as the Confraternity of the Immaculate Conception. The nuns requested that **Da Vinci** paint the figures of baby Jesus, the Virgin Mary, baby John the Baptist, Uriel and depict them on rocks of a cave. Eventually, **Da Vinci** supplied the nuns with his finished piece, but they were horrified. **Da Vinci** had included some un-Christian references that conveyed veiled messages. Entitled Madonna of the Rocks, this painting currently hangs in the Louvre in Paris. The Madonna of the Rocks hid a clue that was described in The Da Vinci Code. Apparently the nuns finally got their wish and **Da Vinci** did a second, milder version, The Virgin of the Rocks. This is the painting that you see before you.

BRITISH MUSEUM

The British Museum has a vast collection of artifacts and art that relates to existing and past cultures, extending over two million years. You could easily spend a day exploring its wonderful collections. Although the museum holds a small amount of Tudor relics, you will be thoroughly impressed by all the other exhibits.

British Museum

Visitor Information
Hours: Sat.-Wed. 1000-1730
Thurs.-Fri. 1000-2030
*Some galleries are open daily, but only at specific times; check to avoid being disappointed.
Closed: Dec. 24-26, Jan. 1, and Good Friday.
Admission: Free
Location: Great Russell Square

Underground: Holborn, Tottenham Court Road, Russell Square
Website: www.thebritishmuseum.ac.uk
We recommend that you check out the website for an extensive
look at the museum's collection.

The Tour

Tudor Period (Room 1)

Dr. John Dee

Dr. John Dee was a true renaissance man: brilliant astronomer,
mathematician, astrologer, alchemist, philosopher, and navigational
expert. In his youth, **Robert Dudley** was tutored by **Dr. Dee**. Anthony
Wood stated in *Athenae Oxoniensis,* that "no one knew **Robert Dudley**
better than **Dee**." Under the reign of **Edward VI**, **Dee** was appointed
Rector of Severn-upon-Severn. While rector, he avidly studied astrology.
He became the court astrologer when **Queen Mary** was in power and
cast horoscopes for **Mary** and her fiancé, **Philip of Spain**. While at court,
Dee befriended **Princess Elizabeth**. She was currently under house
arrest on orders of her sister, **Queen Mary**. **Elizabeth** was fascinated
with astrology and it was alleged, that she not only had **Dee** cast her
horoscope, but also had him compare the sisters two charts. **Dee** was later
taken into custody along with three of **Princess Elizabeth's** servants on
grounds of treason. They were accused of conspiring against the queen
by using enchantments to harm her life. The charges never stuck, so **Dee**
and the servants were later freed.

When **Elizabeth** became queen, her friendship with **Dee** was
rekindled. He was asked to choose a favorable astronomical date for her
coronation. The queen was so intrigued by his astrological predictions
that she had **Dee** instruct her in astrology. He not only became her court
astrologer, but also her "secret agent." He performed confidential missions
for the queen and they developed a secret correspondence code in which
he would use the signature "007." (Yes, the original **James Bond**.) The
00 implied that he was the queen's "secret eyes." In his signature, the
seven is elongated and stretches over the 00s, and may refer to the lucky
number or possibly the square root symbol or the image of spectacles.

Dee was an expert in the field of navigation and was often consulted
by navigators that sailed to the New World. He accurately predicted that
the Spanish Armada would encounter storms as they headed toward the

North Sea while fleeing the British fleet. He wisely advised the British Navy to hang back to avoid the severe weather. England won the war, and the Armada lost a significant number of their fleet during the storm. Some say **Dee** put a curse on the Spanish fleet.

Dee had an extensive library of over 4,000 books, and it was known as the one of the best in Europe. Apparently **Dee** was able to recover some of the ancient books that were strewn around England after the Church Reformation under **Henry VIII**. On occasion, **Queen Elizabeth** would visit **Dee's** home in Mortlake to view his magnificent library and scrying stones. **Dee** used special crystals to "see" and explore the probability of spiritualism. He admitted he didn't possess the mystic talents of crystal gazers and had to employ them for his experiments. He was especially interested in communicating with angels. *The Queen's Fool*, by Philippa Gregory, is an enjoyable book on the topic. **Dee** was the original "wizard," wearing long robes and sporting a long white beard. With his paranormal use of crystal balls, he created a mystical aura and served as a model for several fictional wizards, including **Professor Dumbledore** *(Harry Potter)* and **Gandalf** *(Lord of the Rings)*.

Dr. Dee's Magic

Several objects that **Dee** used for his occult research are on display. Note the two small wax discs, part of a set of four that propped up the legs of his occult table. The biggest wax disc held the shew-stones that seers used to see their visions. The small round shaped crystal is thought to be the chrystallum that seer Edward Kelly used to see his images. The gold disc was also used in Dee's mystical studies.

Dr. Dee's Mirror

This is one of several obsidian mirrors originally used by Aztec priests to summon up visions. **Dee** used this as one of his shew-stones

Medieval Gittern (Room 42)

This intricately-carved musical instrument probably belonged to either **Elizabeth I** or her favorite, **Robert Dudley**. The silver gilt cover on the peg box is inscribed with **Queen Elizabeth's** royal arms and **Dudley's** badge. This is the only remaining significant musical instrument from the Middle Ages.

Tudor Collection (Room 46)

This room contains a variety of artifacts from the Tudor period. A few highlights of this exhibit are the Astrolabe of **Henry VIII**, Seal Burse of **Elizabeth I**, and the Phoenix Jewel.

- **Astrolabe of Henry VIII.** Astrolabes were used to show how the sky would look at a specific place at a given time. **Henry** valued his astrolabe so much that he had it included in one of his portraits.
- **Seal Burse of Elizabeth I.** This velvet purse (burse), embellished with golden strands and silver spangles, held the Great Seal of **Elizabeth I**. Lavishly-stitched in gold are the Royal Arms of England and a Tudor rose flanked by the queen's initials. By stamping her seal in wax, **Elizabeth** approved official documents, proclamations, and public acts.
- **The Phoenix Jewel.** This gold necklace captures a side view of **Elizabeth I**. A green enameled wreath embedded with white and red roses encircles the figure. This represents the unification of the House of York (white rose) and the House of Lancaster (red rose). The other side of the pendant displays **Elizabeth's** personal symbol of a phoenix emerging from a fire, signifying the rebirth of England under her reign.

Rosetta Stone (Room 4)

In 1799, **Napoleon's** soldiers unearthed the Rosetta Stone while enlarging a fort by the town of el-Rashid (Rosetta) in Egypt. The stone came into the possession of Britain through the Treaty of Alexandria in 1801. The discovery of the Rosetta Stone was an important link to understanding the Egyptian civilization and their language. In 196 B.C., a committee of priests wrote a decree on the stone using three different languages: hieroglyphics, Demotic (native language) and Greek. Scholars did not know how to translate hieroglyphics until they had the stone. They were able to use the Greek passage to decipher the hieroglyphics and break the code.

THE BRITISH LIBRARY

The much-admired British Library opened in 1998, after almost 20 years of construction. Here you can find the national collection of books, manuscripts, documents, maps and the National Sound Archives. In addition to being a working library; it includes permanent exhibits that showcase its most valued treasures. This is an exceptional collection and we highly recommend a visit to the library.

Visitor Information

Hours: Mon., Wed. and Fri. 0930-1800
Tues. 0930-2000
Sat. 0930-1700
Sun. 1100-1700
Closed: Holidays
Admission: Free
Address: 96 Euston Road
Underground: King's Cross or St. Pancras
Website: www.bl.uk

The Tour

It is worth a visit to the library just to see the John Ritblat Gallery, which contains its most prized pieces. We've listed just a few of the items that are available to view.

Leonardo's Notebook

This manuscript, referred to as "The Codex Arundel," contains pages of loose papers that **Leonardo** compiled during his lifetime. It contains diagrams and text written in his "mirror writing" style (as in *The Da Vinci Code*).

Shakespeare's First Folio

This book, titled "Comedies, Histories and Tragedies," is the first collected edition of **Shakespeare's** plays.

Alice's Adventures in Wonderland
This is the original book that was creatively illustrated and hand-written by **Lewis Carroll**.

The Tyndale's New Testament
In **Henry VIII's** time, the punishment for owning this book was death. Tyndale had translated the Bible from Greek to English, which gave people who could read the ability to bypass the church for their religious education. Tyndale was tried for heresy and treason; convicted, he was strangled and burned at the stake. His last words were "Lord, open the king of England's eyes."

The Beatles
Included in the library's collection are the original handwritten lyrics to some of the **Beatles** most popular songs, such as "I Want to Hold Your Hand," "Ticket to Ride," and "In My Life." You can also listen to the music on headphones as you view the **Beatle** memorabilia.

Charles Dickens is represented with a copy of *David Copperfield.*

Jane Austen's writing desk is next to an early manuscript that she wrote at age 15.

The Tudors are represented with several documents, including:

- **Sir Thomas More's** last letter to **Henry VIII**.
- A document from **Philip and Queen Mary I** restoring Catholicism as the faith of England.
- **Queen Elizabeth's** response to Council and Parliament regarding marriage and her successor.
- **Edward VI's** diary.

These are just some of the great works that you can see at the library. Check their website for more treasures and for the special exhibits that are showing during your visit.

THE VICTORIA AND ALBERT MUSEUM

The museum holds an extensive collection of objects from the medieval times to the Twentieth Century. Its vast diversity of artifacts has made the museum the world's greatest in art and design. The museum was originally founded in 1852 as the Museum of Manufactures. In 1899, **Queen Victoria** renamed the museum in memory of her husband, Albert. The Tudor period is well represented with items from the reigns of **King Henry VII** to that of **Queen Elizabeth I**. We've included the most significant pieces in the Tudor collection.

Visitors Information

Hours: Daily 1000-1745
Wed. and last Fri. of the month 1000-2200 (only select galleries remain open after 1600; these do not include the Tudor Galleries)
Admission: Free
Underground: South Kensington
Website: www.vam.ac.uk/

The Tour

Gallery 57
Embroidered Panels
While **Mary, Queen of Scots** was held captive, she embroidered these panels. The middle panel was possibly woven for Phillip Howard, the Earl of Arundel, who was also a Catholic that was imprisoned under **Elizabeth's** reign.

Portrait of Mary, Queen of Scots
Mary is seventeen years old at the time this was painted.

Miniature of Mary, Queen of Scots
This portrait was painted while she was imprisoned under **Elizabeth**.

Miniature painting case

In this case are two miniature portraits of **Queen Elizabeth I,** accompanied by a miniature of her favorite, **Robert Dudley.**

The Heneage ('Armada' Jewel)

The regal profile of **Queen Elizabeth** is fashioned in gold. Her picture is encircled with an array of rubies and diamonds.

The Drake Jewel

The naval hero, **Sir Francis Drake,** was given this miniature jewel pendant by **Queen Elizabeth** for his efforts in defeating the Spanish Armada. The jewel contains a small portrait of the queen painted by Nicholas Hilliard. It is richly embellished with rubies and diamonds. The queen's symbol, the phoenix, is also depicted on the pendant.

A Box made for Robert Dudley

This box once held sweets, which was a stylish gift for court members during New Years.

Virginal with devices of Elizabeth I

This instrument was possibly designed for **Queen Elizabeth I.** Within its design is the falcon, her mother's symbol, and also a scepter, a symbol they shared. It is likely **Elizabeth** played this virginal, since she was very a talented musician.

Gallery 58
The Bust of Henry VII

This painted terracotta bust of **King Henry VII** was fashioned from a mold that was made following his death. The artist Pietro Torrigani, who was a fellow student with Michelangelo, also sculpted the Westminster Abbey bronze and marble tomb of **Henry VII** and his wife **Elizabeth.**

Portrait of Henry VIII

This is a royal portrait of **Henry VIII** by an unknown artist.

For detailed descriptions regarding the following three items, refer to the book to the left of the case.

- **Seal Ring with Intaglio.** A ring with the embossed face of **Henry VIII** used to make a wax seal.
- **Miniature Portrait of Anne of Cleves. Henry VIII** based his decision to marry **Anne of Cleves** on portraits he commissioned from Hans Holbein. This was probably painted to help **Henry** with his decision. Holbein's portrayal of **Anne's** beauty was exaggerated. The marriage lasted only six months.
- **Miniature Whistle Pendant. Henry VIII** would hand out expensive tokens such as this for gifts. It is believed that this is the first gift that **Anne Boleyn** received from **Henry**.

Stained Glass showing the arms of Henry VIII and Jane Seymour

This beautiful stained glass piece is thought to come from the Nonsuch Palace that **Henry VIII** built in Surrey. The glass portrays the symbolic red and white Tudor roses, which encircle the arms of **Henry VIII** and **Jane Seymour**.

THE GLOBE THEATRE

The Globe Theatre

On the banks of the Thames lies the highly detailed reproduction of the original Globe Theatre. The theatre has been meticulously recreated just a few yards from where the original Globe once stood. **Shakespeare's** plays are performed from May through September in the open-air theatre just as they were 400 years ago. The plays can be viewed for as little as £5 (for standing), but if you prefer to sit, prices increase dramatically. We were visiting on the day of the final performance of the year; although we were told that the performance was sold out, we decided to check at the box office for any returned tickets. They had just received some returned box seat tickets, which we grabbed. That night we watched Romeo and Juliet performed under the stars. It was truly magical. Since it was the final night of the season, the actors threw out roses to the crowd. Both of us caught red roses from Romeo, something we'll never let our husbands forget. If you are visiting during the performing season, be sure to check for tickets even if it is sold out.

The Globe Exhibition can be viewed year round and masterfully takes the visitor behind the scenes to **Shakespeare's** London and the present-day Globe Theatre. Featured exhibits highlight history, costumes, music, actors and the construction of the Globe. The exhibition is simply fascinating and should be on your agenda. Most of the guides and exhibition workers are actors, so when you ask a question, be prepared not only for the answer, but a little theatre as well. The guided tour is included in your ticket price and lasts approximately half an hour. After the tour, be sure to visit this exhibit and the theatre gift shop.

It is also interesting to note that **Robert Dudley** formed his own acting company, known as the Earl of Leicester's Men, and, in 1574, his acting troop became the first to receive a license from **Queen Elizabeth**. James Burbage, one of the lead actors in **Dudley's** group, built the first playhouse in England and called it The Theatre. He consulted with **Dr. Dee** regarding its design. Burbage went on to build the first Globe Theatre and referenced **Dee's** collection of architectural books for its construction. It is probable that **Shakespeare** used **Dee** as a model for the character Prospero, the sorcerer, in the play *The Tempest*.

Visitor Information

Hours: Oct. 1-Apr. 4
Daily 1000-1700
Apr. 5- Sept. 30
Daily 0900-1200
Closed: Dec. 24, 25
Admission: Buy tickets at the gate; free with Great Britain Heritage Pass.
See Insider Tips for details.
Address: New Globe Walk
Underground: Mansion House, London Bridge
Website: www.shakespeares-globe.org

THE CHARLES DICKENS MUSEUM

The Dickens Museum is actually a house that **Dickens** occupied for two years when he was a young author and newly married. While living at 48 Doughty Street, he finished some of his most famous novels, including *The Pickwick Papers, Nicholas Nickelby* and *Oliver Twist*. The museum holds several artifacts and personal belongings that help recreate the writer's world. This small museum would be most enjoyed by die-hard **Dickens** fans.

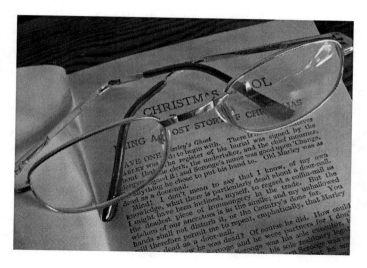

Visitor Information

Hours: Mon.-Sat. 1000-1700
Tues. 1000-1900
Sun. 1100-1700
Admission: Charge
Address: 48 Doughty Street, London
Underground: Russell Square, Chancery Lane, and Holborn; look for signs to direct you.

Website: www.dickensmuseum.com
Check the site for special events.

The Tour

As you enter the museum, you will pass by several ink and wash drawings by Fred Barnard, one of **Dickens'** premier illustrators. Keep going straight down the hall and past the staircase to the small shop to purchase your tickets. You can also enter the enclosed garden from this room. Notice the keystone, (the bearded man) which was once displayed at the entrance of 1 Devonshire Terrace, the house that **Dickens** moved into after Doughty Street (now demolished). This garden area was twice as long when the **Dickens** family lived here.

Go down to the lowest level and enter the library, which is toward the front of the house. During **Dickens'** day this was the kitchen area. The **Dickens** family enjoyed entertaining company and served fine foods and spirits to their guests. **Catherine** even had her own cookbook published. Today, this section holds several versions of **Dickens'** novels. Browse around to find your favorite editions. Don't forget to sign the visitor book before you leave.

Re-enter the hallway, head to your left, and you will be in the Still Room. An extension of the kitchen, this is where bread, butter and tea were prepared. Preserves and cakes were also stored here. Now it is used as a viewing area where you can watch a 30-minute clip on the life of **Charles Dickens**. Next go to the wine cellar; a keg of ale and the wine on the shelves help recreate the **Dickens** cellar.

View the Wash House next. The large copper vat above the small fireplace was the main source of hot water for the **Dickens** household. Mrs.Cratchit used the copper in *The Christmas Carol* to prepare the plum pudding. In the story, the children help Tiny Tim to the Wash House, "that he might hear the pudding singing in the copper." Actually the famous plum pudding was made of raisins, not plums! The copper was mostly used to wash laundry and to heat water for baths.

Upstairs is the morning room, which is the first room to your right down the hallway. This was the back parlor and informal living area and contains several pictures of the family. Samuel Laurence captured the young couple **Catherine** and **Charles** in two separate studies that line the wall. A family tree that begins with **Dickens'** grandparents also hangs on the wall. Next, enter the dining room, where they entertained their guests. A portrait that depicts a young **Dickens** at his desk is displayed above the fireplace. Observe the grandfather clock between the two windows. This once belonged to Moses Pickwick, the owner of a coach shop in Bath. **Dickens** frequented Bath during his days as a young journalist and named Moses as his hero, Samuel Pickwick, in the *Pickwick Papers,* his first novel.

Go up the stairs and you will enter the Drawing Room, which contains several original furniture pieces from the **Dickens** household. The study at the back of the room is probably where **Dickens** wrote his books while living here. The etching called *The Empty Chair* by **Dickens** illustrator Luke Fildes, portrays the great loss that was felt at the time of **Dickens'** death. Below the etching is **Dickens'** original desk. At the right of the fireplace is an unfinished painting titled *Dickens Dream,* which is by R.W. Buss, illustrator of the *Pickwick Papers.* **Dickens** is surrounded by some of the characters he dreamt up. **Dickens** is also seen on his deathbed in a drawing to the left of the window. Now, for a little monkey business! Search the room for the china monkey that **Dickens** insisted was on his desk while he wrote.

On the top floor is the **Mary Hogarth** room. **Mary** was the younger sister of **Dickens'** wife **Catherine**. **Dickens** was obsessed with **Mary**; he held her in his arms when she died in this room and wore the ring from her finger for the rest of his life. No doubt, this obsession with Mary created friction in the marriage.

The Suzannet rooms contain his reading copies of his books, illustrations, letters and playbills. These rooms commemorate his later life as a public orator.

PRINCESS DIANA

The world first became transfixed with **Diana** when, as a teenage pre-school teacher, she started dating **Prince Charles**. Their engagement soon followed, and millions around the world watched as they celebrated their fairy-tale wedding. Following the birth of **Prince William** and then **Prince Harry** (the spare), the fairy tale seemed complete. She was young, beautiful and could relate to the common person as no royal ever had; we were fascinated.

Then the fairy tale began to unravel as she showed us that the royals were not perfect. **Diana's** struggle with bulimia, her marriage, and the "Establishment" (royal inner circle), made her seem more like an average person.

After her divorce, she blossomed into the "People's Princess." She gave a voice to the less fortunate, bringing attention to issues such as AIDS and land mines. Her children were always her main concern, as she tried to shield them from the problems between her and **Charles** and provide them with a normal upbringing.

Her tragic death was a shock and it was hard to believe that she was really gone. People all over the world mourned her passing with the same fascination as they had celebrated her wedding. The following sights, as well as Westminster (previously detailed) are places in London that were important in her life.

Young England Nursery School

Diana was the first **Princess of Wales** that led a "normal" life prior to her wedding. She not only lived on her own in an apartment, she held a job. **Diana** worked as a part-time cook, babysitter, and kindergarten teacher. She was working at the nursery school when she started dating **Prince Charles**.

Underground: Pimlico
Location: St Stavias Hall, St. Georges Square SW1V

Diana's Apartment

Diana's Apartment

At age 18, **Diana** moved into this apartment with three girlfriends. She was working at the Young England Nursery School with pre-school children. **Diana** once said that the happiest time of her life was spent here in this three-bedroom apartment.

Underground: Earl's Court
Location: 60 Coleherne Court, SW5

St. Paul's Cathedral

This is the fourth St Paul's Cathedral to occupy this sight since 604 A.D. The current cathedral was designed by Christopher Wren and was built between 1675 and 1710. This magnificent cathedral is impressive in every aspect, especially the Crossing, with its spectacular dome. Inside the dome, note the Whispering Gallery, where the unusual acoustics allow whispers to echo around the dome. Try it; its fun and really works.

St. Paul's Cathedral

St. Paul's was the beautiful setting for the fairy tale wedding of **Lady Diana Spencer** to **Prince Charles** on July 29, 1981. Over 700 million television viewers watched as **Diana** descended from a glass coach to marry her prince. She ascended the steps to St. Paul's with her 25-foot train flowing behind. Inside the Cathedral, packed with dignitaries from around the world, she captured our hearts as she stumbled over **Charles's** name. She was the first Englishwoman to marry an heir to the throne in 300 years. They left the Cathedral in a coach that **Charles's** brothers had decorated with a sign that read "Just Married."

Hours: Mon.-Sat. 0930-1545
Galleries 0930-1615
Crypt and Ambulatory: 0845-1615
Sun. worship only
Admission: Purchase tickets at the gate;
admission is free with British Heritage pass.
See Insider Tips for more information.
Address: Ludgate Hill EC4
Underground: St Paul's or Mansion Hill
Website: www.stpauls.co.uk

Harrods

Harrods Department Store

Synonymous with London, Harrods is considered a shopping landmark. A trip to London wouldn't be complete without visiting Harrods. It's an incredible store that literally has everything from A-Z. Since the store has over 330 departments, you may want to view their online store guide ahead of time so you can strategically shop. However, you may be in for a little sticker shock, especially with the exchange rate. If you want to buy some inexpensive items to take back with you, explore the food halls on the ground floor for great gifts. We bought candy, biscuits (cookies), and teas to take back home, and they all had the famous Harrods logo imprinted on the package. The overwhelming selection of foods from around the world are beautifully displayed, making the food court our favorite department. After all, a girl's got to eat! Of course you could also dine at one of the several unique restaurants throughout the store, which offer a variety of different cuisines ranging from £8-£12. This beautiful department store, established in 1849, by Charles Harrod, began as a humble grocery store with only two employees. The business prospered due to his philosophy of providing quality merchandise and exemplary service. Today, Harrods is owned by Al Fayed, an Egyptian businessman, who purchased it in 1985. Al Fayed's son, **Dodi**, became involved with **Princess Diana** shortly before her death. After their tragic deaths, Al Fayed dedicated a memorial to them at Harrods. The memorial is found at the bottom of the incredible Egyptian escalator. Ride to the second floor, where you'll see the handprints of Al Fayed's children, which were imprinted during the construction of the escalator. **Dodi's** handprint is located to the left of the entrance to house wares, travel goods, books, and pet shop.

Diana and Dodi Memorial

Visitor Information

Hours: Mon.-Sat. 1000-1900
Closed: Sun. and holidays (open Sundays during Christmas holiday season).
Location: Knightsbridge
Underground: Knightsbridge
Website: www.harrods.com

St. James Palace

St. James Palace is one of London's oldest and most historic palaces. Built by **Henry VIII** in the 1530's, it served as residence of the kings and queens of England for over three hundred years. Although it was not his main residence, **Henry's** mark can still be seen on the palace doorway to the gatehouse, where his initials intertwine with those of his second wife, **Anne Boleyn**.

Queen Mary I, signed the treaty surrendering Calais to France at St. James Palace. She died in the palace from influenza after serving as queen for five years. **Queen Elizabeth I** used St. James Palace as her base during England's battle with the Spanish Armada, receiving messages by fire beacons from Cornwall. **Elizabeth's** prayers were answered; the English ships defeated the Spanish Armada.

After her tragic death in Paris, **Princess Diana's** body was brought to St. James Palace. In the chapel, royal family and friends were able to pay their final respects without the glare of the press that had haunted **Diana**.

Until recently, St. James Palace was the residence of **Prince Charles** (see Clarence House, below). It is currently home to **Princess Anne** and **Princess Alexandra of Kent** and is the official seat of the Royal Court.

Hours: St. James is not open to the public
Underground: Green Park

The Clarence House

King William was the first royal to occupy Clarence house; he lived here after he became king in 1830. More recently, it was home to the **Queen Mother**, from 1953 to her death in 2002. During her engagement, **Lady Diana** spent time here with the **Queen Mother**.

The Clarence House became the residence of **Prince Charles** in August of 2003. He opens it to the public during his summer holiday. On display are items from the late **Queen Mother** and from the Royal Collection.

Hours: Clarence House is open for two months in the summer while Prince Charles is on holiday.
Admission: Charge
Underground: Green Park or St James's Park
Website: www.hrp.uk

Diana Memorial Walk plaque

The Diana Memorial Walk

This was the first permanent memorial to **Princess Diana** following her death. The walk is seven miles long and winds through four of London's most beautiful parks, linking places that were important in the life of **Diana**. The walk is marked by circular plaques that have been set into the walkways. These plaques point the way to the next site on the walk. A wonderful place to start is at her final home, Kensington Palace. Refer to maps C,D, and E to view the walk.

KENSINGTON PALACE

In 1689, **William III** bought Nottingham House and commissioned Christopher Wren to transform it into a palace. After he extended and improved the house, it became known as Kensington Palace and was a favorite residence of the royals until the death of **George II** in 1760. **Queen Victoria** was born at the palace and spent her childhood years here.

Although Kensington Palace is rich in history, it is probably best known for its connection to **Diana, Princess of Wales. Diana** first came to Kensington as the young bride of **Prince Charles**. It was their London home, and where their infant son, **William**, spent the first few months of his life.

After her separation from **Charles, Diana** made Kensington her home and office. She retained **Paul Burrell**, her butler. He and his family occupied Flat 2 in the Old Barracks on the north side of Kensington Palace. In her apartments on the north side of the palace, **Diana** made a home for herself and her sons, **William** and **Harry**.

Following her death, thousands came to Kensington Park to honor **Diana's** memory. The images of flowers, candles and messages spread across the gates of the palace through Kensington Garden, were testaments to the "People's Princess." **Diana's** funeral procession began at Kensington Palace with **Charles**, her children, and her brother following her casket as it was carried to Westminster Abbey, a distance of a little over three miles.

Visitor Information
Hours: Mar.-Oct. 1000-1700
Nov. to Feb.1000-1600
Closed: Jan. 1, Dec. 24-26
Admission: You can purchase tickets at the gate, buy ahead at www.hrp.org.uk, or, with the Great British Heritage pass, it's free. See Insider Tips.

Location: Kensington Palace is located in the west end of Kensington Gardens.
Underground: High Street Kensington
Look for signs to direct you.
Website: www.hrp.org.uk

The Tour

The tour starts with the State Apartments. These rooms were originally built for **King William III** and **Queen Mary II**. **Queen Victoria** restored the apartments to their original splendor and then opened the rooms to the public in 1899. There are several rooms in the tour, but the following are the most noteworthy. The Cupola Room is the most richly decorated, this is where **Princess Victoria** was christened. The original furnishings once used by **Victoria** and **Albert** are displayed in the queen's bedroom. In this room, **Princess Victoria** was notified of her uncle's death, making her Queen of England.

Next visit the former apartments of **Princess Margaret, Queen Elizabeth II's** sister. This area is now an educational center and focuses on its history. As you walk through her apartments, look out the window and notice the Clock Court. This is the courtyard where **Princess Diana** would enter Kensington Palace.

The Royal Ceremonial Dress Collection is probably the highlight of the tour. A large wardrobe of dresses worn by **Queen Elizabeth II** is on exhibit, complete with matching hats. The final room on the tour is where several gowns of **Princess Diana** are on display, along with pictures of her wearing some of the dresses. One of the most recognizable is the black velvet gown that she wore while dancing with **John Travolta** at the White House. This is a truly magical room, bringing back all the fond memories of the extraordinary **Princess Diana**.

Unfortunately, the tour does not include the apartments where **Princess Diana** lived with her sons.

KENSINGTON GARDENS

Kensington Gardens and Hyde Park combine to make the largest of the parks in London. They provide a beautiful oasis where people can relax, exercise and enjoy the arts.

Kensington Gardens was formerly the private grounds of Kensington Palace, but became a public park in 1841, allowing everyone to enjoy the wonderful trees and paths that cover the grounds. We treasured sitting on the benches, relaxing and enjoying the park. One word of caution: do not feed the squirrels. While sitting on a bench behind Kensington Palace, Barb decided to feed a baby squirrel a peanut. Within minutes the squirrel had sent a silent message to all of its friends that there was food. The bench was soon covered in fearless squirrels demanding they also be given peanuts. We were forced to flee, to the amusement of other visitors. Yes, squirrels look cute, but be prepared to either feed them or flee.

Lying west of Kensington Palace is a statue of **Queen Victoria**. This statue was sculpted by her daughter, **Princess Louise**, to commemorate her mother's fiftieth year as Queen of England.

On the south side of the park is a 180-foot tall memorial to **Queen Victoria's** husband, **Prince Albert**. The queen was devastated when her husband died and commissioned this gothic structure that incorporates many different mediums to honor him.

The Serpentine Gallery

The Serpentine Gallery has rotating exhibits of contemporary and modern art. The gallery is located in the south side of Kensington Gardens and is open during exhibitions from 1000 to 1800 daily. There is no admission charge. To see what is showing, go to: www.serpentinegallery.org

Peter Pan Statue

Peter Pan Statue

One of the most beloved statues is the bronze of **Peter Pan**, located to the west of the Long Water. You might remember this statue, featuring **Peter** playing the pipes on top of a tree stump surrounded by animals, in the end of the movie "Hook." **Robin Williams** awakens at the base of this statue. It is fitting that a statue of **Peter Pan** is in Kensington Gardens, since it is where author J.M. Barrie met the Llewelyn Davies children, who were the inspiration for the book about the boy who wouldn't grow up.

The Diana, Princess of Wales Memorial Playground

The playground is located in the northwest corner of the park. Formerly known as the Peter Pan Playground, it was remodeled and named after **Diana** in 2000. In honor of its former name, the playground contains a large pirate ship, tepees, and a mermaid fountain. The park is built to accommodate children of all physical abilities up to age twelve.

The New Diana Memorial

Princess Diana Memorial

Near the Serpentine Gallery is a new memorial fountain honoring **Princess Diana**. The fountain is a large, oval-shaped channel, with water flowing down both sides to a pool at the base. Inside is a large grassy area where one can sit and watch as people enjoy the fountain. It was unveiled July, 2004 at an unbelievable cost of £3.6 million. Unfortunately, the memorial misses its mark in paying proper homage to the remarkable Princess. When we viewed it, our first thought was, "what were they thinking?" **Princess Diana's** mother, **Frances Shand Kydd** commented that it had a "lack of grandeur." **Dodi's** dad, **Mohamed Fayed** came more to the point and indicated that looked like "a sewage works." It is supposed to be an interactive fountain where people can frolic in the water. However, three visitors apparently slipped and were sent to the hospital shortly after it opened. Unfortunately, one of the injured was a child. Prior to the accident, leaves had blocked the filters, causing the fountain to overflow and flood. The fountain has been closed for safety reasons and fenced off, but you can still adequately view this fiasco at the park.

HYDE PARK/ SPEAKERS' CORNER

The Marble Arch

Kensington Gardens blends into Hyde Park in the east. **Henry VIII** claimed Hyde Park from the monks of Westminster Abbey in 1536. It was used as a hunting ground for **Henry** and his court. **Charles I** opened the park to the public in 1637, creating a retreat from the city.

Every Sunday morning since 1872, when the citizens of England won the right of free assembly, people have come to Speakers' Corner to voice their opinions. The site is fitting since it is close to where thousands were hung at Tyburn (close to the Marble Arch). Before they were executed, prisoners were allowed to say what they thought. The tradition continues today (without the hangings), where anyone who has an opinion can speak his or her mind. So grab a soapbox and say what you feel, joining the ranks of Lenin, Marx, and other impassioned individuals, or listen to the hecklers that revel in mocking the speakers.

If you find yourself by Lancaster Gate, stop by our favorite pub, The Swan. This is where prisoners, on their way to their execution at Tyburn, were able to get off the wagon and have a final drink. Hence, the phrase "back on the wagon," referring to the end of their drinking days.

BUCKINGHAM PALACE

Buckingham Palace

Buckingham Palace became a royal residence when **George III** bought the home of The Duke of Buckingham for his wife, **Queen Charlotte**, renaming it the "Queen's House." When their son, **George IV**, inherited the home in 1820, he hired John Nash to convert it into a palace. The staterooms remain unchanged from Nash's original design. Unfortunately, **George IV** died before the reconstruction was complete.

When **Queen Victoria** moved to Buckingham Palace in 1837, it became the official London residence of Britain's Monarch. She renovated the palace, adding a magnificent ballroom and moving the Marble Arch entrance to the northeast corner of Hyde Park.

Today, the palace serves as both home and office for **Queen Elizabeth**

II and her husband, **Prince Phillip**. There are over 600 rooms in the palace, including the state apartments, where Her Majesty greets and entertains guests.

Possibly the most famous part of the palace is the front balcony, where the Royal Family makes a public appearance following moments of both celebration and somber events. The Royal Family gathered on the balcony after the wedding of **Prince Charles** and **Princess Diana**. The image of their first kiss as husband and wife was telecast around the world.

Diana lived at Buckingham Palace after becoming engaged to **Prince Charles**. During her stay at the palace, **Diana** became friends with one of the queen's personal footmen, **Paul Burrell**. As the queen's footman, **Paul** occupied a room in the palace with a wonderful view down the Mall. As you face the palace, you can see his room, below the broad triangular gable, the fourth window from the left. **Paul** left Buckingham Palace and service to the queen to become butler to **Prince Charles** and **Princess Diana** at their country estate, Highgrove. After their separation, **Paul** became **Diana's** butler, living in the old barracks at Kensington Palace until her tragic death.

On its way to Westminster, **Princess Diana's** funeral procession passed by Buckingham Palace. It was hard to believe that only sixteen years had elapsed since **Diana** had come to Buckingham Palace as the **Princess of Wales**.

Visitor Information

Hours: The State Apartments of the palace are open for two months in the summer while the queen is on holiday. Hours are from 0930-1730, with admissions every 15 minutes.
Admission: To view current dates and purchase tickets, visit www.royal.gov.uk.
Tickets may also be purchased at the ticket office in Green Park at Canada Gate from 0900-1600.
Visitor's entrance to the palace is on Buckingham Palace Road, which is on your left as you face the front of the palace.
Changing of the Guard:
May-Aug. daily at 1130

Sept.-Apr. alternating days at 1130
Underground: Victoria, St James Park or Green Park; all require short walk to palace.
Website: www.royal.gov.uk

The Tour

The tour of the palace includes nineteen lavishly-furnished staterooms filled with priceless works of art and ornate furniture. It's hard to imagine that this is not a museum, but a working part of the palace where the Royals entertain their guests. A walk through the gardens is also included in the tour, where you can see some of the thirty-nine acres behind Buckingham Palace.

Among the many state apartments is the Throne Room, which, during **Victoria's** reign, was a place for dancing and court gatherings. This splendid room, decorated in scarlet and gold, is where the chairs used at **Queen Elizabeth's** coronation in 1953 are located.

Queen Victoria added a ballroom during reconstruction of the palace. This magnificent room, the largest in London, opened in 1856 to celebrate the end of the Crimean War. Today this room serves many functions: State banquets, concerts, the yearly diplomatic reception and investitures.

The State Dining Room is used for more informal meals. Many presidents, prime ministers, and other distinguished guests have dined here, surrounded by state portraits of kings and queens of England.

To celebrate her upcoming coronation in 1838, **Queen Victoria** held the first State Ball in the Blue Drawing Room. Thirty imitation onyx columns, created by John Nash, decorate the Blue Drawing Room, along with a porcelain table that was made for **Napoleon**.

The three eldest children of **Queen Elizabeth II** as well as **Prince William**, son of **Princess Diana** and **Prince Charles** were christened in the Music Room with water from the River Jordan. Originally planned as a library for **George IV**, the Blue Dining Room is where guests are presented to the queen during state visits.

Perhaps the grandest of all the State Rooms is the White Drawing Room. The gold walls highlight the delicate colors of the French antiques, and elegant glass-cut chandeliers hang from the ornate ceiling. It is where the queen and members of the Royal Family gather prior to official occasions. If your visit is during opening times, it is definitely worth your while to visit the palace.

THE QUEEN'S GALLERY

The Queen's Gallery is located on the west side of Buckingham Palace where a chapel once stood. The chapel, built during Queen Victoria's reign, was destroyed in a German bombing raid on September 13, 1940.

A conservatory was constructed on the site and, in 1962; **Queen Elizabeth II** and **Prince Phillip** converted it into the Queen's Gallery. Exhibits are based on different themes involving over 9,000 pieces of art from the Royal Collection. Past exhibits have included the works of Leonardo da Vinci, Vermeer, Michelangelo and other great artists.

The gallery was recently reopened after renovation and expansion, with three and a half times more space for exhibits on the upper level. The lower level has rooms for education and lectures.

The Queen's Gallery is the sight of one of our more hilarious adventures. As usual we became chatty with the guards, and one informed us of a special visit from Princess Alexandra that was going to take place within the next half hour. We were not sure who she was, but the guard explained that she was **Queen Elizabeth's** cousin. When we entered the next room, we began a conversation with the guard that was on duty, and being "in the know," we casually mentioned Princess Alexandra's visit. She was appalled that we knew this "secret information" and asked us how we knew this! We both sheepishly looked away, and she knew we would not reveal our source. She then exclaimed she had a pretty good idea who the guard was. She eventually warmed up to us as we kept her busy with other questions. When the princess arrived, the guard gave us a nudge. We both tried to inconspicuously glance at the princess, as we kept talking to the guard and watched the princess move throughout the room as she examined the exhibit. When she left the room, we decided to leave, satisfied we had seen royalty. We thanked the guard and we proceeded on our way out. As we were leaving the gallery, I spied the princess one more time and I pointed my finger and said, "There's the Princess! I was actually pointing to her reflection in the mirrored walls;

the princess was standing right behind me. Thankfully, she was deep in conversation and didn't notice my blunder. However my sister broke out laughing and we giggled our way down to the coat check. What made it even funnier was the woman guard, who had quietly pointed out the princess to us, was also down there. It was hard to contain our laughter, but we thanked her again and didn't reveal our secret encounter with the princess. As we have said, get to know the guards and, who knows, you may encounter a princess too!

Visitor Information

Hours: Open daily 1000-1730
(Last admission, 1630)
Closed Apr. 9, Dec. 25, 26
Admission: You can purchase tickets at the gate, buy ahead at www.royal.gov.uk, or
with the Great British Heritage pass, it's free. See Insider Tips for more information.
To see what is currently showing on exhibit, visit their website.
Underground: Victoria
Website: www.royal.gov.uk

THE ROYAL MEWS

Royal Mews coach

The Royal Mews, designed by John Nash in 1825, houses the Royal Family's ceremonial coaches, limos, and horses.

The Royal Family owns over 100 coaches and carriages, with some of the most ornate on display in the Royal Mews. The stunning Gold State Coach has been used in every coronation since 1821. Weighing four tons, it requires eight horses to pull it. The coach is decorated with symbols of England that are gilded in 22-carat gold.

The Glass Coach is used in all royal weddings. **Diana Spencer** rode in the Glass Coach to St. Paul's Cathedral for her wedding to **Prince Charles**. **Queen Victoria** bought the Irish State Coach for the ride to the opening of Parliament and it is still used for that purpose to this day.

Following their wedding, **Prince Charles** and **Princess Diana** rode in the 1902 State Landau from St. Paul's Cathedral to Buckingham Palace.

The two breeds of harness horses used to pull the carriages and coaches are Cleveland Bays and the Windsor Greys, chosen for their stamina and mild temperament. You'll be able to view the impressive working stables that house these royal horses. The horse stalls are immaculate and have beautiful tiled walls and nameplates. There is also an impressive collection of saddles, harnesses and riding uniforms, some items even date back to the 18th century. The horses are exercised daily at the riding school, a large arena located near the entrance. The Mews also serves as the Royal Garage, housing the royal motorcars. Included in the fleet of autos are the Rolls-Royce limousines with clear tops, which allow the royals to be seen by the public.

Visitor Information

Hours: Late Mar.-late Sept.
Daily 1000-1700
Late Sept.-late Oct.
Daily (except Fri.) 1100-1600
Please note that it can close on short notice based on the queen's needs.
Admission: Purchase tickets at the gate. Buy ahead at www.royal.gov.uk;
free with the Great British Heritage pass. See Insider Tips.
Underground: Victoria
Website: www.royal.gov.uk

THE DA VINCI CODE

I f you've read the Da Vinci Code, you will enjoy seeing some of the places visited by **Langdon, Sophie** and **Teabing.** Along with the following sights, be sure to include Westminster Abbey and The National Gallery to trace their journey.

King's College London

King's College has a worldwide reputation for teaching and research. Within the college's Religion Department is the Research Institute in Systematic Theology, a cutting-edge religious research library. Take our advice and do not ask the theology secretary where the research library is located. It seems there have been quite a few others who have asked her this question and she has grown quite testy regarding *The Da Vinci Code.* The research library is not within the main King's College buildings which are located on the Strand, but at the Maughan Library just up the road.

The Maughan Library

In the Da Vinci Code, **Langdon** and **Sophie** came to the Research Institute in Systematic Theology hoping they could use the library's complex computer to find where the pope was interned and find **Teabing.** The room that is described in the book is actually found within the college's Maughan Library. Obviously, **Sophie** and **Langdon** had fake college ID's, since one needs official college identification in order to enter the college library. The library is located north of Fleet Street on Chancery Lane, opposite the Law Society. This is just up the road from the Temple Church. You may view only the outside of the library.

Address: The Strand, School of Humanities
Underground: Temple
Website: http://www.kcl.ac.uk/

The Temple Church

The Temple Church

The Temple Church was built by the Knights of Templar. The Church has two parts, the Round and the Chancel. The Round was finished in 1185 and is one of the few round Churches that remain in England. Inside you will find life size stone effigies of Templar Knights. **Teabing**, **Sophie** and **Langdon** entered the church trying to solve the riddle, "In London lies a knight a Pope interred." After they realized it was the wrong place, **Teabing** was taken hostage by **Remy**. **Robert** and **Sophie** were then in a race to save **Teabing** and solve the mystery.

Hours: Generally open Wed-Sun
Address: Inner Temple Lane (see map)
Underground: Temple
Website: www.templechurch.com
The Church has irregular hours; to get current information, contact the Verger at Verger@templechurch.com.

Opus Dei London

This is the London Headquarters of Opus Dei, the deeply devout Catholic sect, with offices worldwide. Note that the number five marking the address of the headquarters of the Opus Dei has been removed from door. However, you can see the faint outline of the Roman numeral five, denoting where it had once been. This was pointed out to us by a friendly Opus Dei priest that just happened to be walking by. **Silas** went here after the confrontation at the Temple Church. The police caught up with him, shooting both **Silas** and the **Bishop**. **Silas's** body was later found in nearby Kensington Gardens.

Opus Dei Headquarters

Hours: Not open to the public
Address: 5 Orme Court
Underground: Queensway

Horse Guards Parade

Built in 1745 to house the old palace guard, the Horse Guards Parade is London's largest single open space and is the location for the Changing of the Guard. It is located across from St. James Park, London's oldest and smallest park. This is where the **Teacher** instructed **Remy** to park the limousine. Later the **Teacher** slipped **Remy** a drink laced with peanuts, causing an allergic reaction that killed him.

Address: Whitehall

Underground: Westminster

THE BEATLES

I magine there's no **Beatles**, I wonder if you can?" That would be an impossible task for most baby boomers, since the Fab Four shaped our lives in so many ways. Beginning with their uplifting pop songs and ending with more introspective pieces, the **Beatles** guided us through the turbulent sixties and continue to touch our lives. No wonder the **Beatles** are considered the number one band of all time! So put on your "Rubber Souls," head toward "Abbey Road," and prepare to take a "Magical Mystery Tour," tracing the steps of **John, Paul, George** and **Ringo.**

Abbey Road Studios

Abbey Road Studios

The Beatles had their picture taken as they crossed the street in front of the studio. Traffic was stopped and the camera was placed at the top of a ladder in the street. After you cross Abbey Road, go to the entrance of the studios, where you can have your picture taken at the top of the stairs. In these studios, on June 6, 1962, the **Beatles** had their audition with **George Martin**. He told them what he thought they needed to do and then asked them if there was anything they didn't like. **George Harrison** replied that he didn't like **Martin's** tie. It was a good thing that **Martin** had a sense of humor; he signed the **Beatles** and they went on to become the biggest band in history. Their first record, "Love Me Do," and ninety percent of their songs were recorded in studio two at Abbey Roads Studios. **Beatles** fans still leave notes on the wall that lines the front of the studio, be sure to bring a marker so you can leave your special message to the boys.

If you'd like to be seen crossing Abbey Road, send your friends to the web cam at http://www.abbeyroad.co.uk/virtual_visit/webcam/ and let them know when you'll be there.

Underground: St. John's Wood

Exit tube to Finchley Road. Cross Finchley Road and follow Grove End Road to the crossing of Abbey Road. To your right is the crossing from the cover of Abbey Road. This is a busy intersection; remember to look to your right before crossing.

Abbey Road Café

If you take a left as you exit the underground you will see the Abbey Road Café. Along with coffee this tiny store offers Beatles merchandise.

Underground: St. John's Wood

Paul's House 7 Cavendish Avenue

Paul bought this house in 1965 when he was dating **Jane Asher**. They lived here until their breakup. **Paul** kept the house and fans flocked here to see him. One fan broke in through a window, inspiring the song "She Came in Through the Bathroom Window." He still owns the house and stays here occasionally while in London.

Underground: St John's Wood

From tube stop, cross both Finchley Road and Grove End Road, follow Wellington Road to Circus Road and turn right. Take left on Cavendish Avenue to 7 on right hand side.

From Abbey Road Studios: Continue down Grove End Road, past

the monument in the middle of the road to Circus Road, which will be on your left. Follow Circus Road to Cavendish Avenue; take a right to 7 on the right side of the road.

Paul's House

Apple Records – The Roof Top Session

This was one of the offices for Apple Records, a company started by the **Beatles** to help artists just starting in the world of entertainment and arts. It was a great idea, but a financial disaster. Many of the "artists" who came to Apple had little or no talent, taking advantage of the free food, drinks and money. A few had talent, including a young man named **James Taylor**, who recorded "Carolina on my Mind" here.

The **Beatles** recorded "Let it Be" at the studio and performed a live concert on the rooftop on January 30, 1969. People crowded the streets, trying to figure out where the music was coming from. The police were called, stopped the performance, and then allowed them to play their final song, "Get Back." This was the last live performance given by the **Beatles**.

Underground: Piccadilly Circus

From tube stop, head north on Regent street to Brewers Street, take a left following Brewers Street to Savile Row and take right to 3 Savile Row

The Prince of Wales Theatre

In this theatre, the **Beatles** played the Royal Command Performance in front of the **Queen Mother** and **Princess Margaret** in 1963. This is an annual charity event with very expensive tickets. It was in front of this crowd that **John** said "For our next number, I'd like to ask for your help. Will those in the cheaper seats clap your hands? The rest of you just rattle your jewelry."

Underground: Piccadilly Circus

From tube stop, follow Coventry Street; the theatre is on the right hand side.

The Indica Art Gallery
(currently the James Hyman Fine Art Gallery)

On November 9, 1966, **John Lennon** was invited by a friend to a preview at the art gallery. The exhibit was showcasing a Japanese artist named **Yoko Ono**. One of the exhibits was a stepladder leading up to a magnifying glass hanging from the ceiling. **John** climbed the ladder and looked through the glass to see the word "Yes." Another was called "Hammer A Nail In." **John** wanted to pound a nail into the artwork, but **Yoko** said she didn't want the art disturbed before the opening. After negotiations, **Yoko** said he could pound in a nail for five shillings. **John** offered her an imaginary five shillings to pound in an imaginary nail. **Yoko** smiled, and the rest is history.

6 Mason Yard

Underground: Piccadilly Circus

From the tube stop, follow Piccadilly Road west to Duke Street. Turn south (left) and proceed down the street past Jermyn Street to small alley on the left (as soon as you see Chequer's Tavern). You will enter Mason Yard and the gallery is located at this site.

The Indica Art Gallery

The Scotch of St. James
(Now the Director's Lodge Club)

The **Beatles** were regular visitors at this club, even having their own table at which no one else could sit. The first live performance of the **Jimi Hendrix** Experience was held here.

13 Masons Yard

To the right of the Indica Art Gallery

Ringo's Flat 34 Montagu Square

The Chicago Tribune called **Ringo's** flat the "Ultimate Rock 'n Roll Pad" due to the number of rock stars that passed through its door. **Ringo** first leased the flat after marrying **Maureen** in 1965. Soon after, their son was born and they decided to move to a house, keeping the flat for friends to use. For a short period, **Paul** put a recording studio in the basement for artists to record. "Eleanor Rigby" was one of the songs he worked on here.

Chas Chandler, former bass player for the Animals, had recently discovered **Jimi Hendrix** in New York, and persuaded him to move to London. They, along with their girlfriends, were the next occupants of the flat. They ended up trashing the flat, reportedly painting the entire place black. **Ringo** not only asked them to leave, but also sued them for damages.

John and **Yoko** moved into the flat after **Cynthia** (**John's** wife) returned from vacation, discovered **Yoko** in their home, and kicked them out. The pictures of them naked on their album "Two Virgins" were taken in the flat. After the police busted **John** and **Yoko** for possession at the home, **Ringo** was forced to give up the flat.

Underground: Marble Arch

Follow Oxford Street west to Edgware Road, take right to Seymour Street then left on Seymour Place, then right on Montagu Place.

M.P.L.—Paul's London Office

McCartney Productions, Ltd. is one of the largest privately-owned music publishing companies in the world. **Paul** had wanted to use the Abbey Road Studio, but found it already booked, so he created an exact replica of Abbey Road Studio 2 in the basement.

Underground: Tottenham Court Road

Cross Oxford Street and follow it west to Soho Street. Take a left into Soho Square and turn right to 1 Soho Square.

Royal Albert Hall

Affectionately known as the "Nation's Village Hall," the Royal Albert Hall has hosted over 150,000 events since it opened in 1871. Some of its varied performances include classical concerts, ballet, opera, ballroom dancing, poetry and rock concerts.

The **Beatles** first played here on April 18, 1963 in the BBC sponsored "Swinging Sound 63," along with some other acts. **Jane Asher** was in the audience on assignment for "Radio Times," a magazine which highlighted the BBC listings. After the concert **Jane** was able to go backstage and meet the **Beatles**. She was later invited to join them at their hotel, which sparked the start of **Jane** and **Paul's** lengthy romantic relationship. The Rolling Stones were also attending the concert that evening. They had just met the **Beatles** a week before, when the Stones were performing at the Crawdaddy Club. The **Beatles** had heard about the group and wanted to check them out. After the Stones' performance, the two groups met. Later, the Stones invited the **Beatles** back to their apartment for a party. The **Beatles** gave them backstage passes and tickets for their upcoming show at the hall. The next time the **Beatles** played at Royal

Albert Hall was September 1963 for the Great Pop Prom. This time the **Beatles** were featured, along with the Rolling Stones.

Although the **Beatles** performed as a group only twice at the Royal Albert Hall, they continued their appearances individually. **George** performed a concert in 1992, supporting the Natural Law Party. **Ringo** was a special guest at his concert and joined in on "Roll over Beethoven." **John** and **Yoko** made quite a statement when they appeared together in December, 1968, emerging from a white bag for an avant-garde type festival. Their act was entitled "Alchemical Wedding." **Paul** has made numerous appearances, but the tribute concert for **Linda** was probably the most touching. Organized by friends Chrissie Hynde and Carla Lane the "Here, There and Everywhere" concert raised funds for **Linda's** animal charities. Another tribute, A Concert for **George**, marked the first anniversary of the beloved **Beatles** death. Eric Clapton hosted the event and was joined by Ravi Shankar, Tom Petty, Joe Brown, **Ringo**, **Paul** and numerous other friends of **George**. Dhani, **George's** only child bears a striking resemblance to his father and played guitar during the concert. **George's** wife Olivia remarked to **Paul**, "Seeing Dhani on stage it looked like **George** stayed young and we all just got older." This concert is on DVD and is wonderful to watch.

Royal Albert Hall was built by **Queen Victoria** after the death of her husband, **Prince Albert**. The prince had been motivated by the success of the 1851 Great Exhibition in Hyde Park, to build a series of permanent structures in order to house events that would enlighten the public. His idea progressed slowly, and he died in 1861, before his vision was realized. The queen not only built the grand hall in memory of her prince, but also the colossal monument that lies directly across the street. A gold leaf statue of **Prince Albert** is enshrined by an immense ornate pavilion.

Tours are available at Royal Albert Hall. You will be able to view the auditorium, peek inside the queen's box, access the Royal Retiring Room and learn about the hall's history. Tours are given Fridays through Tuesdays, 1000-1530, from door 12. There is a charge and the tours are on a first come, first serve basis. To view details about Royal Albert Hall's tours, cost and hours, visit their website.

Website: www.royalalberthall.com

Underground: High St. Kensington, Knightsbridge

Hard Rock Café

The restaurant serves the regular burger and fries fare, but contains great memorabilia from rock and roll history. Even if you're not hungry, go to visit the vault in the gift shop across the street. It's free and contains many items, including **John Lennon's** glasses, army jacket, and hand-written lyrics for "Imagine." It's a hands-on museum, so go ahead and touch! We are both huge **Beatles** fans and it was amazing to touch the actual army jacket that **John** wore. **John** has always been my favorite **Beatle**, so my sister captured the moment with a flash of the camera. We had come in at the tail end of the tour and most people had left. One person was still strumming a Hendrix's guitar and some girls were sitting on Jimi Hendrix's sofa. Of course we started talking with the guide and soon we were sitting on Jimi Hendrix's couch having a tea party with **John Lennon's** tea set from India!

On Jimi's Couch with John Lennon's tea set

Restaurant Hours: Mon.-Thurs. 1130-midnight
Fri.-Sat. 1130-1a.m.
Open daily for breakfast 0800-1100
Store and Vault hours: Sun.-Thurs. 0900-1230 a.m.
Fri.-Sat. 0900-1a.m.
Address: 150 Old Park Lane
Underground: Hyde Park Corner

Marylebone Railway Station

The movie "A Hard Days Night" opens with the boys running down Boston Place to the station. As they're running down the street, **George** accidentally trips. Although this wasn't in the script, the director liked it and kept it in the movie. They run into the front of the station and hide in telephone booths, which now are, unfortunately, gone. After the boys return from their train ride, they are mobbed by fans. They run into a car and leave the station through the archway at the end of the station.

Underground: Marylebone

London's Beatle Store

This small shop is filled with fun **Beatles'** memorabilia, but it seems to be a bit overpriced. If you're looking for that hard-to-find **Beatle** collectable, this might be the shop for you.

Underground: Baker Street Station
Hours: Daily 1000-1830
Address: 231 Baker Street
Website: http://beatlesstorelondon.co.uk/

The British Library

A must-see for any Beatles fan, see section on British Library.

The Original London Walks

They have guided tours of **Beatles** sites and a lot more. Check them out at http://www.walks.com .The colorful and entertaining Richard Porter is the official Beatle guide and the author of the *Guide to the Beatles' London*. You can purchase his book at the end of the tours. Even if you aren't a **Beatles** fan, check out the many walks offered through Original London Walks; accept no substitute.

OTHER SITES OF INTEREST

The London Eye

Each of the 32 capsules of this giant observation wheel offer full views of the city as they rise 450 feet above the banks of the Thames River. Built to celebrate the Millennium, the London Eye has quickly become one of London's major attractions. Since we both suffer from a fear of heights, we have not ridden the Eye for worry that our screams will dampen the experience for others. For those of you that don't suffer from acrophobia, the Eye is a wonderful way get a bird's-eye view the city and beyond. If you would like to ride the Eye, you should book your tickets ahead of time to guarantee a ride and avoid long lines.

The London Eye

Hours: Feb- Apr 0930-2000 May-Sept 0930-2100
July-Aug 0930-2200 Oct-Dec 0930-2000
Closed: Christmas Day and for yearly maintenance early Jan. to
beginning of Feb.; please see website.
Admission: Buy tickets at gate or ahead on website
Underground: Waterloo or Westminster
Website: www.londoneye.com

Madame Tussauds

From rock stars to royalty, Madame Tussauds has them all. Wax
figures of famous people through out history can be found here. Madame
Tussaud learned her trade by making death masks of famous victims of the
French Revolution. The very guillotine that beheaded Marie Antoinette
can be seen, in the Chamber of Horrors, which portrays the most grisly
criminals and the crimes they committed. You can also visit the Spirit
of London, showcasing significant events in the history of London. If
celestial stars are what you like, Madame Tussauds offers the London
Planetarium for your viewing pleasure. Be sure to bring your camera so
you can have your picture taken by these wax wonders. Strike the pose
by Madonna; pretend to hobnob with the queen, or better yet, bop with
the **Beatles**, yeah, yeah, yeah!

Hours: Weekdays 0930-1730 Weekends 0900-1800
During Feb. half term, see website.
Closed: Christmas Day
Admission: Buy tickets at gate or ahead on website
Underground: Baker Street
Website: www.madame-tussauds.com

The Imperial War Museum

Although a war museum seems odd in a women's travel guide, this
museum not only shows the machinery of war, but also the impact of
war on society. The massive entry contains airplanes, missiles, and the
even interior of a submarine. After viewing these impressive machines,
go to the displays that illustrate the altered lives of a society at war.
Some of the many exhibits include surviving air raids, understanding
propaganda, and rationing. One of the most emotional and memorable
exhibits is the Holocaust exhibit, which contains artifacts and personal
memorials of what occurred during this horrible time. It is something

you will never forget. Visit their website to see what special exhibits are on during your visit.

Hours: Open 1000-1800
Closed: Dec. 24-26
Admission: Free
Underground: Lamberth North, Elephant & Castle, Waterloo
Website: www.iwm.org.uk

The Cabinet War Rooms

Far beneath the city streets of London lies the incredible Cabinet War Rooms. This is where Winston Churchill and his cabinet met to decide their plans for WWII. They lived in these secret rooms and planned their strategies for the campaign; this location was known to only a very few select top officials. At the end of the war the rooms were left as they were when the cabinet heard the news of their victory. Even the pins in the maps, books and charts show the position they occupied at the end of the war. The recently opened Churchill Museum is now included in the exhibit. This museum is dedicated to Churchill's public and private life. Both museums are included in the price of admission.

Hours: Daily 0930-1800; last admission 1700
Closed: Dec. 24-26
Admission: Charge at gate
Underground: Westminster or St. James
Website: http://cwr.iwm.org.uk

SHOPPING

Art

Every Sunday from 1000 to 1800, over 250 artists display their original works of art, offering everything from abstracts to traditional, on the fence railings located on the north side of Kensington Gardens and Hyde Park. This is a wonderful way to spend a Sunday afternoon; take our word for it, you don't want to miss this experience. If you're hungry, pop across the street to The Swan for some great fish and chips.

Selfridges

If fashion is your passion, this store is for you. Cutting-edge styles and fashion-forward clothing are synonymous with Selfridges. At first glance, you will be lured in by the lavish window displays. Although the exterior is distinctly classical, don't be fooled; the interior is uniquely contemporary and is in sync with their innovative and progressive attitude. Once inside, you will be one of 30,000 daily customers that browse their unique items. Furniture, cosmetics, electronics, chic fashions, and sporting goods are among the million plus products they carry. You may want to please your palate at one of seventeen bars and restaurants located throughout the store. If you're a princess that needs to be pampered, try their luxurious day spa for the ultimate indulgence.

American born founder Gordon Selfridge was a true retail visionary. He once worked at the Chicago-based Marshall Fields stores and was credited with the ideas of creating annual sales and a bargain basement. In 1909, Selfridge opened his first store in London on Oxford Street. Always one step ahead of his competitors, he offered a huge selection of unique merchandise, restaurants, a library, a silence room (intended for reflection), and many other conveniences that were meant to make shopping an enjoyable experience. The expression, "the customer is always right" first came from Selfridges lips. He was also fond of saying "Selfridges is for Everyone." This still rings true, as both bargain hunters and upscale shoppers are clientele. Some of their accolades include Retailer of the Year—Visit London, Top in Cool—Leaders Awards, In Style—Best Department Store in London. Your woman's intuition will tell you that Selfridges is *the* place to shop in London.

Hours: M-W, Fri-Sat 10.00-20.00
Thurs 10:00-21:00 Sun 11.30-18.00
Address: 400 Oxford Street
Underground: Bond Street
Website: www.selfridges.com

Harvey Nicholas

This posh department store is a favorite of the affluent and famous. High-end fashions from chic established designers such as Yves Saint Laurent, Stella McCartney, Gucci, and Versace are displayed as well as creations from new and upcoming designers. For a complete list of fashion designers, refer to their website. Fabulous furniture, exquisite jewelry, the latest perfume and beauty products, fine restaurants and stylish bars are also part of this elegant ultra-modern store. If food is your craving, their swanky food hall will satisfy your desire.

Harvey and Nick's, a pet name for the regulars, was a favorite shopping destination for **Princess Diana**. She would head there on her "Pamper Diana Days," as she referred to them. Noting her Harvey habit, **Prince Charles** severed his account with the store once their divorce was in the works.

Hours: M-F 10:00-2000
Sat 10:00-1900 Sun Noon-1800
Underground: Knightsbridge, Hyde Park
Website: www.harveynichols.com

Fortnum and Mason

Established in 1707, Fortnum and Mason is considered one of London's premier luxury department stores. This exquisite store has a reputation for unsurpassed quality and service. Elegant chandeliers, grand fountains, and beautiful murals lavishly showcase their fine merchandise. A highlight is their impressive food hall boasting of caviar, pastries, truffles, exotic fruits, wines, British farmhouse cheese, cured meats and fish. For souvenirs, consider their large selection of authentic English fare; teas, chutney relishes and preserves. Fortnum and Mason are probably best known for their famous hampers, which display their specialty items in handmade wicker baskets sporting their logo. Fashion, perfumes, household articles, crystal, china and four elegant restaurants occupy their six shopping floors. For a more detailed description of their shopping line, refer to the store guide on their website.

The **Beatles** would buy their groceries from this pricey store for Apple Records. Free food and drink were available to the many "artists" that frequented the studio. Apple's extravagant and unmonitored spending habits eventually created a financial mess for the company.

The royals have been linked to Fortnum and Mason from its beginning. Co-founder William Fortnum was a former footman for **Queen Anne**, but had a side business as a grocer. He prospered with his store, always flaunting his royal connections. His grandson Charles served under **Queen Charlotte** and again business seemed to flourish, given the royal ties. **Queen Victoria** often ordered their delicious dishes for court functions. She was so impressed that she issued Royal Warrants, which allowed Fortnum and Mason to endorse their products with the official seal and use special phrases such as, "By appointment to Her Majesty, **Queen Victoria**." Today **Queen Elizabeth** and **Prince Charles** continue the royal patronage and are supplied with their specialty goods by appointment. So if you're feeling like a queen today and want to sample the fine food the royals prefer, Fortnum and Mason should be on your regal agenda.

Hours: Mon.-Sat. 1000-1830 Sun.1200-1800
Underground: Piccadilly Circus or Green Park
Website: www.fortnumandmason.com

Marks and Spencer

This store is more of a mainstream department store rather than upper crust. You'll notice countless Marks and Spencer stores throughout the streets of London. Fashion for the family, household items, furniture, cosmetics and all the basic essentials can be found at M&S. The food halls are fabulous and can't be beat. To avoid the lunch rush, we recommend that you get there early. You might want to grab some grub for a picnic in Hyde Park at their Kensington location. **Princess Diana** frequented this M&S for their wonderful muffins.

Website: www.marksandspencer.com

Regent Street

The curvaceous stretch of upscale and specialty stores on Regent Street will tempt the shopper in you. Whether you're in the mood to power shop or just browse, this sweeping selection of stores will appeal to your shopping urges. Regent Street hosts a number of notable shops including the Liberty Department Store, Hamley's (toys), Lilywhites (sport shop), Burberry and Austin Reed. Other favorites include Next, Laura Ashley, Lacoste and the Apple Store. For shoppers that desire a little coffee perk, a Starbucks awaits you. The best selection of stores lies between Oxford Circus and Piccadilly Circus, which is approximately ¾ of a mile long. To view these areas store by store visit http://www.streetsensation.co.uk/regent/rs_intro.htm .

John Nash was commissioned by the Prince Regent (later George IV) to build a boulevard to connect his residence in St. James Park to Regents Park, where Nash was to build a palace. Nash completed the street in 1825; however the palace was never built, due to insufficient funding. Yet, Regent Street proved to be an important link in the London infrastructure, reducing traffic in the Strand and Charing Cross areas. Another function of the boulevard was to create a division between the affluent Mayfair district and the lower class Soho. This well-defined class division still exists today. Mayfair is ritzier, while Soho has a trendy feel. Currently, most of the buildings date back to the1920's and are not original to Nash's time; however his initial vision of a beautiful winding boulevard remains intact.

Harrods

For the ultimate London shopping experience, you can't miss Harrods. See **Princess Diana** section for all the details.

Transport Museum Shop

Adjacent to the museum is a fun shop filled with clothing and souvenirs decorated with underground sayings and logos. We have bought Mind the Gap t-shirts and boxer underwear that display the underground map. It's a great place to pick up items that are unique to London. It is located in the Covent Gardens Piazza.

Hours: Daily1000-1800 except Fri. 1100-1800
Underground: Covent Gardens
Website: www.ltmuseum.co.uk/

Oxford Street

To shop at large chain stores and discount shops, visit Oxford Street, located between the tube stops of Marble Arch and Tottenham Court Road.

Covent Gardens

This indoor-outdoor market is filled with specialty shops and boutiques, promising a unique shopping experience. Street entertainers add to the festive atmosphere. To get there, take the underground to Covent Gardens tube stop.

Next

If you're looking for trendy clothes that any teenage boy or girl would love, visit Next. We have bought several outfits for our children at their stores. You'll find Next stores all around London and at the Gatwick airport. There are twenty-one locations in London.

Kings Road

Located in Chelsea, this road is lined with upscale stores, unique boutiques, and restaurants. After shopping, stop into the Chelsea Kitchen for great food at very reasonable prices.

Heathrow and Gatwick Airport Shopping

We love shopping at the airport because it's tax-free and we can always find that last-minute gift. Harrods stores are available at both airports. We have purchased affordable wool scarves at the Tie Rack. You have to be at the airport early, so you might as well use this time to shop and spend those leftover pounds. For a complete list of all shops available at both airports, visit www.baa.co.uk/main/airports/heathrow or www.baa.co.uk/main/airports/gatwick.

CHEAP EATS IN LONDON

St. Martin-in-the-Fields (Café in the Crypt)

I n the basement of St. Martin-in-the-Fields Church, located across from Trafalgar Square, is a unique cafeteria-style restaurant serving authentic English food. We highly recommend the soups, sandwiches and especially the bread pudding!

Hours: Mon.-Sat 0800-1830 and Sun. 0800-1900.
Underground: Charing Cross.

The Liberty Bounds

Located close to the Tower of London, this cute pub offers a variety of inexpensive food that includes wraps, sandwiches, burgers, and main meals. Second floor is non-smoking and window seats offer great views of the Tower.

Address: 15 Trinity Square (kitty corner from the northwest section of the Tower)
Underground: Tower Hill

The Chelsea Kitchen

The charming Chelsea Kitchen offers simple dining, excellent soup and reasonably priced lunches. A serving of hearty soup costs about one pound, lasagna or pizza dish is £2, and main courses cost £4-6. Fixed price menu costs about £6, and, if you're really hungry, a three course meal runs around £8.

Hours: Mon.-Sat. 0800-2330; Sun. 0900-2330.
Location: 98 Kings Road
Underground: Sloane Station

Sticky Fingers

Not exactly a cheap eat, but really fun if you're a Rolling Stones' fan. Their menu includes American and European cuisine. Sticky Fingers has been voted as having the best burger in London.

Hours: 1100-2300 daily
Address: 1A Phillimore Gardens.
Underground: High Street Kensington

The Hard Rock Café

This is the original Hard Rock Café, with memorabilia that will blow away rock and roll fans. If you're in the mood for a little taste of home, the Hard Rock offers burgers and fries, along with your typical American fare. Be sure to visit the Vault across the street to enjoy the hands-on exhibit.

Restaurant Hours: Mon.-Thurs. 1130-midnight
Fri.-Sat. 1130-1 a.m.
Open daily for breakfast 0800-1100
Store and Vault hours: Sun.-Thurs. 0900-1230 a.m.
Fri.-Sat. 0900-1 a.m.
Address: 150 Old Park Lane
Underground: Hyde Park Corner
Website: www.hardrock.com/

The Swan

Our favorite pub features great fish and chips and wonderful Kronenbourg beer on tap. It's not cheap, but you can't beat the friendly staff, piano bar, and relaxing atmosphere. Pick out your bench under the heat lamps on the patio as you enter. Tell them Polly and Barb sent you!

Hours: Mon.-Sat. 1000-2300
Sun. 1000-2230
Address: 66 Bayswater Road
Underground: Lancaster Gate

The Orangery

Situated just to the north of Kensington Palace, the Orangery was originally built as a greenhouse for **Queen Anne** in 1704. This beautiful restaurant now serves light lunches and teas on white linen tablecloths. A great place for a special treat with the girls!

The Orangery

Hours: 1000-1800 Mar.-Oct.
1000-1700 Nov.-Feb.
Closed: Dec. 24-26
Lunch served 1200-1500
Tea served after 1500
Location: Kensington Gardens
Underground: Kensington High Street

Chain Restaurants: Available throughout London, offering quick meals for low prices.

- **Benjy's**—featuring low-priced sandwiches and snacks.
- **Pret a Manger**—offering tasty sandwiches
- **Tesco Metro**—small supermarket featuring pre-made, low-cost sandwiches

Grocery Stores

It is also wise to check where the nearest grocery store is located. We often go there not only to stock up on snacks, but purchase meals, wine and beer. Note: if you plan on buying wine or beer, be sure to bring your own bottle openers, we had a hard time finding them. If you truly want to save on your budget, this is the way to go. Not only will you save money, you'll enjoy seeing the variety of English foods that are not commonly found in American grocery stores. You will also note many familiar American brands and items that have British logos and packaging designs.

INSIDER TIPS

The following travel tips will help you prepare for your journey abroad. Our helpful hints cover basic items you may want to bring, transportation options, special discount passes for theatre and exhibits, currency, VAT tax information, safety concerns, contacting home and weather information. We also provide some great travel resources that offer some additional information and tips.

Things to Pack

Pack light and casual. Bring two pairs of comfortable walking shoes. If you want to stand out as an American tourist, bring white tennis shoes and colorful clothing! To dress like a Londoner, pack black, only black. Be sure to take an umbrella and rain gear. It is a good idea to bring layers of clothes, since the weather fluctuates from day to day. Throw in a scarf and put light gloves into the pockets of your jacket. We recommend backpacks and find they are the most comfortable way to carry your belongings while sightseeing. We also both use a money belt for our credit cards and currency.

We strongly advise bringing a converter and not just an adapter for your electrical appliances. We learned this the hard way when Barb burned off her bangs in Oslo with Polly's curling iron. (Thanks Polly!) Fortunately, Barb still had a little fringe of bangs left, but it could have been worse! Our room reeked of singed hair and the odor hung in the air our entire visit. Once we left Oslo, we were on our way to visit some of our mother's thirty-six first cousins in Sweden, and they, of course, snapped many pictures of all of us, including Barb and her beautiful new bangs. In Britain the standard electrical voltage is 240V AC, 50HZ. Converters change the electrical current to the proper voltage for your appliance. **Adapter plugs do not convert electricity,** but are necessary so dual voltage appliances, converters and transformers can be plugged into various wall outlets around the world. Basically, you will need an adaptor so your appliance can be plugged into the wall and a converter if your appliance is not dual voltage. We have been lucky enough to stay in some hotels in London that have outlets that are 120 V, which is standard voltage in the United States. Look under hotel amenities, which may list voltage.

We always bring some favorite snacks from home and carry them with us while sightseeing. The small twist top bottles of water and the little six oz. cans of pop (pack these in your carry on bag only) are great to bring with you. Buying bottled water and pop becomes costly; note that diet pop tastes different in Europe. We always throw some snacks and small beverages in our purse before we head out each morning.

Flight Tips

When you check in at the airport, be sure to ask if the flight is full. If the plane is not full, you may be able to switch your seats, so you have a row to yourselves. On the other hand, if the plane is overbooked, you could get bumped to the next flight and may be offered money, free miles or a free trip for your trouble. We have come close, but haven't been able to take advantage of this little bargain, but we always check!

Most of us "really" look forward to the airline food that will be served on the flight. Remember, most airlines do accommodate special diets. Polly usually calls ahead and orders the veggie meals. Our sister Lynn got wind of this and was inspired to inquire about free-range chicken. Save yourself a phone call; free-range chicken is not served on airplanes.

We only travel in lowly coach class, but have been pleasantly surprised by this little perk; wine and drinks are free on some overseas flights! But don't indulge too much; you have some serious sightseeing to do once you land in London.

When traveling on the airplane, we recommend using inflatable pillows that will support your neck while you're sleeping. It is also important to get up and walk around while on the plane to minimize swollen feet. The seemingly ridiculous exercise videos shown during the flight are actually good for you, so flex those feet! Wear loose fitting shoes on the plane, because no matter what, your feet will swell.

Getting to London from the Airport

Heathrow Airport

There are several transportation options to choose from. The least expensive option is the underground; it will take roughly sixty minutes to arrive in central London. You can purchase your ticket at the airport, or if you have a pre-paid travel card or voucher zones one through six for the underground, there is no additional cost. (See below for travel card information.) Although some of tube stations have elevators or escalators, most have steep stairs that you will have to navigate with your luggage. We have done this before with our seventy-year-old mother and she's never forgiven us, even though we carried all her bags. It's not a bad way to get into London depending on how much luggage you have brought and number of tube exchanges to your hotel.

The National Express is a bus service that runs from Heathrow to central London and takes up to one hour and forty minutes. See web site www.nationalexpress.com, then click on airports, select Heathrow, and enter London as your destination. It will list all the stops available in central London.

The Heathrow Express is a non-stop train that runs from Heathrow to Paddington station, departing every fifteen minutes. It takes fifteen minutes to go from Heathrow to London on the express. The train is expensive, and the best deal is found by purchasing a return (round trip) ticket. For further information on the Heathrow Express, visit www. heathrowexpress.com.

Airport shuttle service is also available and will bring you directly to your hotel. A little more expensive than the train, the shuttle provides door-to-door service, which eliminates extra cab fare or additional tube stops. Discounted fares for large groups are also offered. It is customary to give your driver a 10% tip. Check out these websites www.london-airport-shuttle.com/, www.adlg.co.uk/tariff.htm, www.london-airport-transfer.com for additional information.

Cabs are also available, but they are extremely expensive, considering the cheaper options we described. Make sure your cab is licensed and plan to tip your driver ten percent of the fare.

Gatwick Airport

There are several transportation options available from Gatwick airport to central London. It is important to note that underground transportation from Gatwick to London is not available.

The National Express, a bus service that runs from Gatwick, could take up to one hour and twenty minutes to reach central London. See website www.nationalexpress.com, click on airports, select Gatwick, and enter London as your destination. It will list all the stops available in central London.

Three train options are available from Gatwick airport to London. The Gatwick Express is the most expensive and fastest, with journey time being thirty minutes between Gatwick and London-Victoria. Their website is www.gatwickexpress.com. Thameslink trains travel from Gatwick to London Bridge in thirty-five minutes at half the price of the express. When using the Thameslink train, you can choose from these five London train stops: London Bridge, Black Friars, City Thames Link, Farringdon and Kings Cross-Thameslink. Refer to www.thameslink. co.uk/ for more information. The Southern railway takes thirty-five minutes and the fare is comparable to the Thameslink lines and travels from Gatwick to Victoria Station. To learn more about this option, visit www.southernrailway.com.

Airport shuttle service is available and will bring you directly to your hotel. The shuttle offers door-to-door service, which eliminates extra cab fare or additional tube stops. Discounted fares are offered for large groups. It is customary to give your driver a tip of ten percent of the fare. Check out the following websites: www.london-airport-shuttle. com/, www.adlg.co.uk/tariff.htm and www.london-airport-transfer.com .

Cabs can also take you directly into London, but it is the most-costly option. Make sure the cab is licensed, and plan on tipping 10% of the fare to your driver.

Traveling Around London

The underground or "tube" is the best way to get around London. There are many tube stations throughout London, creating easy access to all the sights. Some of the lingo you need to know is "mind the gap," which refers to the gap in between the train and the pavement. Sometimes it's a little wide and you may need to hop on or off. A female voice recording reminds you to "mind the gap," just in case your mother isn't with you. Also, look for the signs that say "Way Out," which is not some hippie phrase, but a sign indicating the way out of the station. Some stations are pretty drab, while others are distinctly decorated. Some of our favorites include Victoria Station with its old world charm, and Paddington Station, where you can purchase the famous bear. Be prepared to go the wrong way on the tube a few times. We still do this, but you can easily get back on the right track, so don't panic! One of our favorite memories was during rush hour traveling with our mother. We were packed in like sardines, barely being able to see one another. After a few stops, Polly finally realized we were going the wrong way and we had to maneuver ourselves out at the next stop. Once we were out and able to breathe again, we able to laugh about our blunder.

The ticket attendants are helpful in pointing people in the right direction, so use them if you are unsure of which way to travel. Another important tip is to keep your tube pass in a handy spot. You will need it to enter and exit each time you use the tube. Our mother always travels with a purse that has a million zippers and we were constantly searching for her tube pass. Out of warranted frustration, we overruled our mother and put her tube pass in our pocket.

When purchasing your tube pass, you may want to consider buying the Visitor Travelcard, which is the most efficient and inexpensive way to get around London. **Visitor Travelcards cannot be purchased in London. Be sure to purchase them ahead of time.** There are two types of cards that are available for purchase in three, four and seven day passes. The central zone card is the least expensive; it covers underground and most bus transportation within central London, zones one and two. You will be able to get to all the sites we have listed in our book, with the exception of Hampton Court and Windsor Castle. The all-zone card covers underground, most buses, and some trains within zones one through six as well as train rides to Hampton Court. With this travelcard, you will need to purchase an extension ticket in order to visit Windsor Castle. If you arrive at Heathrow airport, you can use the all-zone card for the underground into London. Unfortunately, the card is not valid on the trains from Gatwick. We have always purchased the Visitor Travelcard when visiting London.

The Visitor Travelcard can either be purchased as a voucher or as a ticket. The voucher is redeemable at the following London Transport Travel Information Centers: King's Cross, Oxford Circus, Liverpool Street, Piccadilly Circus, St. James Park, Heathrow Terminals 1, 2 and 4, Euston, Hammersmith, Waterloo, Victoria and Paddington. The ticket is the actual Visitor Travelcard that you can use immediately upon arrival. For further details about the Travelcard voucher, refer to http://railpass.

com/britrail/passes/lvtc.htm. Information concerning the Travelcard ticket can be accessed form www.ticket-on-line.com.

Theatre

London theater rivals Broadway and we highly recommend catching at least one show. The half-price ticket booth (TKTS) makes London theatre affordable. They accept credit cards, cash, and debit cards. The ticket booth is located at the clock tower building in Leicester Square (north of the Portrait Gallery). The booth is open Mon.-Sat. 1000–1900, Sun. 1200-1530. Only day-of-performance tickets are sold.

There are other discount ticket shops located outside of the Leicester Square tube station. Be sure to check if they are members of STAR (The Society of Ticket Agents). Ask for the cost of their booking fees, the price printed on the ticket, and where the seats are. Do not buy from street vendors; the tickets could be counterfeit. You may also purchase your tickets at the theatre, but you will pay full price. To view the current showings of performances, go to www.officiallondontheatre.co.uk . Unless there is a show that you absolutely must see, buy your tickets in London, not ahead of time.

The British Heritage Pass

If you are planning to visit a number of the sights that we've mentioned, you may want to consider purchasing the British Royal Heritage Pass to save money. The pass includes free entrance to Hampton Court, Windsor Castle, The Queen's Gallery, The Royal Mews, Kensington Palace, and half-price admission to the Tower of London, among other sights. Purchase this ticket ahead of time; otherwise, you can buy the pass at the Britain and London Visitor Centre at One Regent Street in London. You can order your ticket at www.raileurope.com/ (go to British Products and then scroll down to the pass); however, there are several sites you can visit to purchase this pass.

Currency

Twenty Pound Notes

By using your credit card, you will be able to get the best exchange rate. There are very few places that do not accept major credit cards. We use our credit cards for almost all of our purchases while in London. Retailers now have an option to charge more for services and goods bought with credit cards; however they must clearly display information on the price difference. If you want to have some British currency for buying small items, consider using an ATM debit card from your local bank. You might be charged a small transaction fee from your bank and also a charge from the ATM in London. A fee is charged for every transaction you make, so be sure to withdraw enough money to save on the withdrawal fees. Check with your bank for the fees that would apply to you. If you prefer to bring traveler's checks, exchange them at banks, larger post offices, bigger travel agencies, and building societies (similar to banks) and some tourist information centres. Usually banks are open from 0930-1630 on weekdays. On Saturdays, some banks will be open all day. A few banks are even open on Sundays. Do not exchange at airports, hotels, and the Bureaux de Change, which all charge exorbitant fees. To find out what the current rate for conversion from U.S. dollars to British Sterling, visit www.xe.com/ucc/.

You'll notice that British currency doesn't offer a one pound note; their smallest bill is the five pound. The one and two pound coins not only weigh down your wallet, but quickly add up to quite a chunk of change. When paying for items, be sure to use your change and not just the paper currency.

Tipping

This is a general guide for a customary tip:

- **Restaurants:** You will find that some restaurants have already included a service charge in the bill. If it is not already included, a tip of 10-15% is customary.
- **Porter:** It is appropriate to tip 50-75 pence per suitcase.
- **Taxis:** It is customary to tip 10-15% of the fare.
- **Hairdressers:** A tip of £2 is suggested.

VAT Tax

Included in the price of most goods that you buy in Britain is a 17.5% VAT tax (Value Added Tax). You are eligible for a refund on VAT tax on purchases above £50-100 per transaction, but check on individual stores for their limit. Stores displaying the "Tax Free Shopping" sign participate in the program. The VAT form must be completed and validated at the store of purchase in order to get a refund. VAT refunds only refer to goods taken out of Great Britain and do not pertain to services. You must present your goods, receipts, and passport at the airport customs office to receive your refund. Remember to have all these items handy in your carry-on luggage. Be prepared to stand in line up to a half an hour. After your paperwork has been officially stamped, you will have four ways to receive your refund. You can go to the Cash VAT refund desk and get your refund in British Sterling (for possible airport shopping) or you can convert to United States currency; (due to the conversion, you will lose money). You'll receive the most bang for your buck by choosing the credit card refund by mail option (you'll need a British stamp). The worst choice is to receive a refund check in British Sterling, which requires conversion fees in the United States. It may take up to three months to get your credit card refund.

Safety Tips

Although we consider London a safe city for women travelers, we recommend these following safety tips:

- Pickpockets frequent tube stations and tourists areas, so be more aware in these surroundings.
- Use a money belt to keep your passport, credit cards and the majority of your money safe.
- Make a few copies of your passport before you leave; keep one in your luggage, give one to a travel partner and leave a copy at home.
- Keep your passport locked in a safe in your room and carry a copy with you.
- At night, stay on well-lit and crowded streets. Avoid being the only ones at a tube station or traveling in a rail car.
- Only use licensed, metered cabs. **Do not** use minicabs, which may not be insured or licensed, and where cab fares are sometimes negotiated and not metered. More importantly, there have been reports where women passengers have been harmed by some minicab drivers.
- If you prefer to phone for a cab, dial +44(020)72720272, which will cost you approximately $5 extra.
- Ladycabs, driven only by women, are also available at +44(020)7254 3501.

We have never had any safety concerns while traveling throughout London, but we keep these tips in mind and use our common sense.

Contacting Home

To contact home, purchase telephone cards in post offices, newspaper stands, and many bureau de change stations. We have found that it is much easier to use these phone cards instead of the ones you can purchase in the United States. We usually don't call home from our hotel room, since they usually charge quite a bit for an international call. Locate a pay phone to make your calls. To call the United States, first dial 001 and then your phone number. Check with your hotel to see if it offers email services or use the many internet cafes throughout the city to email home. With the time difference, this is an excellent way to keep in touch with friends and family.

Weather

The winter temperatures are moderate with highs ranging from the 40's to 50's. This is a great time to sightsee, since the crowds are low. We have not traveled to London during the summer because prices are high and crowds are at their peak. If you do decide to go during the summer, be sure to inquire about air conditioning because it is not standard.

We have included the following charts to help you plan for your journey and to use once you arrive in London:

Average London Temperature

Jan L: 35 H: 47	**May** L: 46 H: 61	**Sept** L: 50 H: 66
Feb L: 35 H: 45	**June** L: 51 H: 68	**Oct** L: 44 H: 66
Mar L: 37 H: 50	**July** L: 55 H: 72	**Nov** L: 39 H: 57
Apr L: 39 H: 55	**Aug** L: 53 H: 71	**Dec** L: 27 H: 47

Celsius to Fahrenheit conversion table

°C	°F	°C	°F	°C	°F
36	96.8	23	73.4	11	51.8
35	95.0	22	71.6	10	50.0
34	93.2	21	69.8	9	48.2
33	91.4	20	68.0	8	46.4
32	89.6	19	66.2	7	44.6
31	87.8	18	64.4	6	42.8
30	86.0	17	62.6	5	41.0
29	84.2	16	60.8	4	39.2
28	82.4	15	59.0	3	37.4
27	80.6	14	57.2	2	35.6
26	78.8	13	55.4	1	33.8
25	77.0	12	53.6	0	32.0
24	75.2				

Helpful Hints

Talk with the locals to find out about pubs, restaurants, and markets in your area. We have learned so much from Londoners about their city. Guards at museums and palaces have a wealth of knowledge and have always been excited to share their expertise. Police officers are very willing to help you. Your trip will be enriched if you take the time to chat with the people you meet.

Keep left but look right! You may know that Brits drive on the left side of the street. So it's important for pedestrians to look to their right before crossing a street to avoid being hit by a vehicle. You will begin to notice that Brits also walk on the left side of the walkway. To avoid walking against the flow, you should walk on the left side on sidewalks, stairs, and when crossing the street.

Journeywoman: The Premier Travel Resource for Women

This free online travel magazine is just for the girls! An outstanding site that offers female oriented travel tips, women travel tales, free newsletters and several other excellent travel resources. As far as kudos, they were voted the best online travel magazine by the North American

Travel Journalist Associations. Some of their featured departments include gal-friendly city sites, love stories, journey doctor, travel 101, women helping women travel, girl talk guides, and she shops worldwide. For information that is London-specific, key into their search engine. www.journeywoman.com

Visit Britain

If you have any questions regarding your trip, contact Visit Britain at 1-800-462-2748 or www.visitbritain.com. The people at Visit Britain are travel authorities and are anxious to help you with the simplest of questions, free of charge. Even if you don't have any questions, call them for free brochures, maps, and a list of special events that will take place during the time of your visit. We use and highly recommend these helpful people.

You Go Girl Website

Visit our website for updates on London travel. Also, if you'd like to pass on your travel experiences, recommend a book, or share travel insights, visit us at www.yougogirltravelguides.com.

We hope that you have found our book informative and helpful, but most of all fun. Have an incredible journey "across the pond," exploring the sights that you've read about with "the girls!" Have a jolly good time and **You Go Girl!** Cheers!

Even though the boys may try anything to go, remember this trip is just for the girls!

MAP INDEX

Featured Sights   Maps

Eateries

Shopping

Underground	Maps
Angel	B
Baker St	A
Bank	F
Barbican	B
Bayswater	C
Blackfriars	F
Bond	D
Borough	F
Cannon Street	F
Chancery Lane	B,E
Charing Cross	E
Covent Garden	E
Earl's Court	C
Edgware Road	A
Elephant and Castle	F
Embankment	E
Euston Square	A,B
Euston Station	A,B
Farringdon	B
Gloucester Road	C
Goodge Street	A,B
Great Portland Street	A,B
Green Park	D
High Street Kensington	C
Holborn	B,E
Hyde Park Corner	D
Kings Cross	B
Knightbridge	D
Lambeth North	E
Lancaster Gate	C,D

Underground	Maps
Leicester Square	E
Liverpool Street	F
London Bridge	F
Mansion House	F
Marble Arch	D
Marylebone	A
Monument	F
Morningston Crescent	A,B
Nottinghill Gate	C
Oxford Circus	D
Paddington	A,C
Picadilly Circus	E
Pimlico	E
Queensway	C
Regents Park	A
Russell Square	B
Sloane Square	D
South Kensington	C
Southwark	E,F
St. James Park	E
St. John's Wood	A
St. Pancras Station	B
St. Paul's	F
Temple	E
Tottenham Court Road	B,E
Tower Hill	F
Victoria Station	D
Warren Street	A,B
Waterloo	E
West Brompton	C
Westminster	E

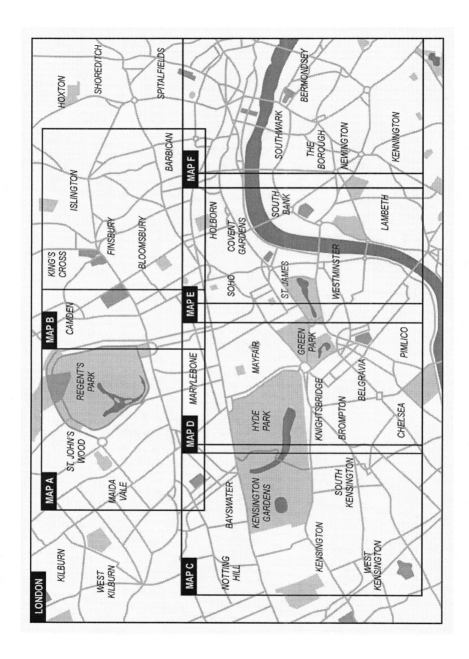

LONDON

MAP A
MAP B
MAP C
MAP D
MAP E
MAP F

KILBURN
WEST KILBURN
ST. JOHN'S WOOD
MAIDA VALE
REGENT'S PARK
CAMDEN
ISLINGTON
HOXTON
SHOREDITCH
SPITALFIELDS
KING'S CROSS
FINSBURY
BLOOMSBURY
BARBICAN
MARYLEBONE
NOTTING HILL
BAYSWATER
KENSINGTON GARDENS
HYDE PARK
MAYFAIR
SOHO
HOLBORN
COVENT GARDENS
ST. JAMES
GREEN PARK
WESTMINSTER
SOUTH BANK
SOUTHWARK
BERMONDSEY
THE BOROUGH
NEWINGTON
KENNINGTON
LAMBETH
KNIGHTSBRIDGE
BROMPTON
BELGRAVIA
PIMLICO
CHELSEA
KENSINGTON
SOUTH KENSINGTON
WEST KENSINGTON

152

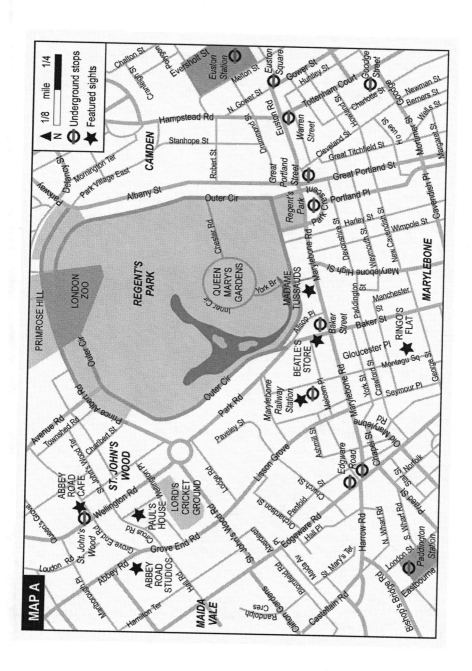

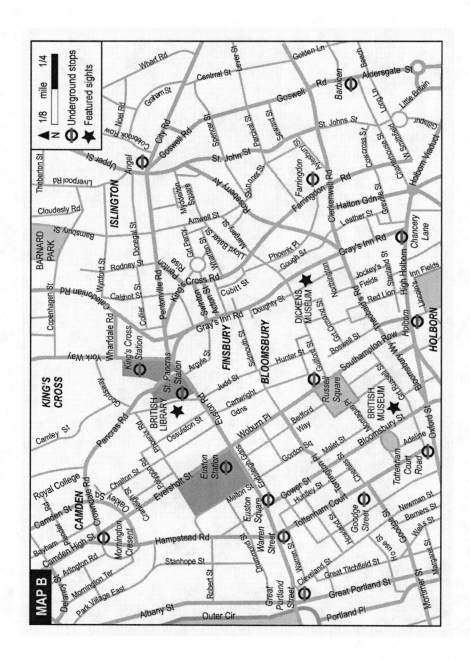

MAP B

N

1/8 | mile | 1/4

Ⓤ Underground stops
★ Featured sights

ISLINGTON

BARNARD PARK

KING'S CROSS

FINSBURY

BLOOMSBURY

HOLBORN

CAMDEN

King's Cross Station

St. Pancras Station

BRITISH LIBRARY

Euston Station

DICKENS MUSEUM

Russell Square

BRITISH MUSEUM

Lincoln's Inn Fields

Barbican

Wharf Rd
Central St
Graham St
City Rd
Goswell Rd
Noel Rd
Colebrook Row
Upper St
Liverpool Rd
Theberton St
Cloudesly Rd
Barnsbury St
Copenhagen St
Caledonian Rd
Wynford St
Rodney St
Donegal St
Calshot St
Collier
Pentonville Rd
Penton Rise
King's Cross Rd
Amwell St
Myddelton Square
Great Percy St
Lloyd Baker St
Margery St
Roseberry Av
St. John St
Skinner St
Percival St
Seward St
Spencer St
Goswell Rd
Goswell Rd
Lever St
Golden Ln
St. Johns St
Aylesbury St
Clerkenwell Rd
Farringdon Rd
Farringdon St
Halton Gdn
Leather St
Greville St
Chancery Lane
Gray's Inn Rd
Phoenix Pl
Gough St
Cubitt St
Gray's Inn Rd
Swinton
Acton St
Wharton St
Doughty St
Jockey's Fields
Northington
Theobald's Rd
Red Lion
High Holborn
Holborn
Lincoln's
Concross St
Charterhouse St
W. Smithfield
Holborn Viaduct
Aldersgate St
Little Britain
Giltspur
Beech
Long Ln
Cowcross St

Copenhagen St
York Way
Wharfdale Rd
Goodsend
Rawstorne
Camley St
Pancras Rd
Royal College
Camden St
Bayham
Camden High St
Camden Crescent
Mornington Crescent
Delancy St
Arlington Rd
Mornington Ter
Park Village East
Albany St
Outer Cir
Stanhope St
Robert St
Hampstead Rd
Chalton St
Churchway
Ossulston St
Euston St
Euston Rd
Midland Rd
Pancras Rd
Phoenix Rd
Oakley Sq
Crowndale Rd
Eversholt St
Plymouth St
Drummond St
Melton St
Euston Square
Warren Street
Cleveland St
Great Portland Street
Portland Pl
Great Portland St
Great Titchfield St
Howland St
Goodge St
Goodge Street
Tottenham Court Road
Tottenham Court Rd
Gower St
Huntley St
Gordon Sq
Malet St
Chenies
Gower St
Torrington St
Byng Pl
Southampton Row
Bloomsbury
Great Russell St
Bloomsbury Way
Adeline
Oxford St
Newman St
Berners St
Wells St
Mortimer St
Margaret St
Judd St
Cartwright Gdns
Woburn Pl
Bedford Way
Hunter St
Guilford St
Great Ormond St
Boswell St
Sidmouth St
Argyle St
Stanhope Row
Red Lion

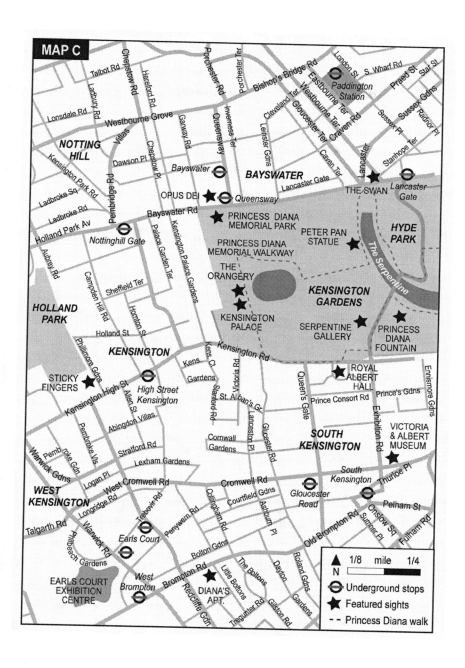

MAP C

Talbot Rd
Chepstow Rd
Hereford Rd
Ladbury Rd
Lonsdale Rd
Westbourne Grove Villas
Porchester Rd
Porchester Ter
Bishop's Bridge Rd
London St. S. Wharf Rd
Eastbourne Ter
Paddington Station
Praed St. Star St
Sussex Gdns

NOTTING HILL
Kensington Park Rd
Dawson Pl
Chepstow Pl
Garway Rd
Queensway
Inverness Ter
Leinster Gdns
Cleveland Ter
Gloucester Ter
Westbourne Ter
Craven Rd
Craven Ter
Lancaster Ter
Sussex Pl
Radnor Pl
Stanhope Ter

Bayswater
BAYSWATER
Lancaster Gate
Ladbroke Sq.
Ladbroke Rd
Pembridge Rd
OPUS DEI ★⊖ Queensway
THE SWAN Lancaster Gate

Holland Park Av
Nottinghill Gate
Palace Garden Ter
Kensington Palace Gardens
Bayswater Rd
★ PRINCESS DIANA MEMORIAL PARK
PETER PAN STATUE ★
HYDE PARK

Aubrey Rd
Campden Hill Rd
Sheffield Ter
Horton St.
PRINCESS DIANA MEMORIAL WALKWAY
THE ORANGERY ★
★
KENSINGTON PALACE
KENSINGTON GARDENS
SERPENTINE GALLERY ★
★ PRINCESS DIANA FOUNTAIN
The Serpentine

HOLLAND PARK
Holland St.
KENSINGTON
Kensington Rd
Kens. Ct
Gardens
Kens. Victoria Rd
St. Alban's Gr.
Stanford Rd
Lancaster Pl.
Queen's Gate
★ ROYAL ALBERT HALL
Prince's Gdns
Ennismore Gdns

STICKY FINGERS ★
Phillimore Gdns
Kensington High St
Allen St.
High Street Kensington
Abingdon Villas
Stratford Rd
Cornwall Gardens
Gloucester Rd
Prince Consort Rd
SOUTH KENSINGTON
Exhibition Rd
VICTORIA & ALBERT MUSEUM ★

Pembroke Vls.
Lexham Gardens
Collingham Rd
South Kensington
Thurloe Pl
Pelham St.

WEST KENSINGTON
Warwick Gdns
Logan Pl
Pembroke Rd
West Cromwell Rd
Longridge Rd
Cromwell Rd
Courtfield Gdns
Ashburn Pl
Gloucester Road ⊖
Onslow Sq.
Sumner Pl
Fulham Rd

Talgarth Rd
Warwick Rd
Trebovir Rd
Penywern Rd
Earls Court ⊖
Bolton Gdns
Old Brompton Rd

Philbeach Gardens
EARLS COURT EXHIBITION CENTRE
West Brompton ⊖
Brompton Rd
Redcliffe Gdn
DIANA'S APT. ★
Little Boltons
The Boltons
Tregunter Rd
Dayton
Roland Gdns
Gilston Rd
Gardens

▲ N 1/8 mile 1/4
⊖ Underground stops
★ Featured sights
- - Princess Diana walk

155

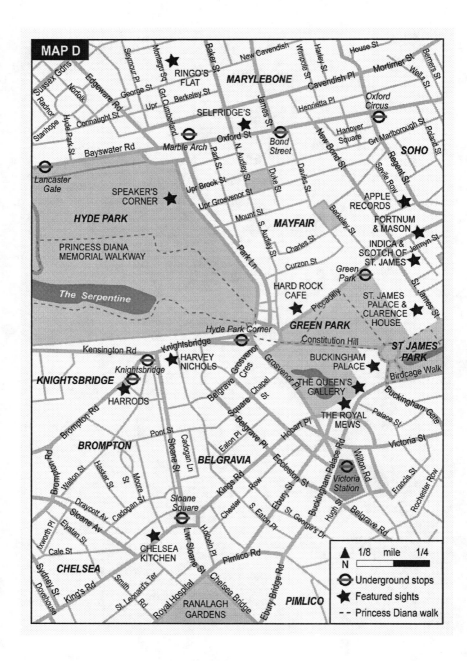

MAP D

RINGO'S FLAT
MARYLEBONE
SELFRIDGE'S
Oxford Circus
Marble Arch
Bond Street
SOHO
Lancaster Gate
SPEAKER'S CORNER
APPLE RECORDS
HYDE PARK
FORTNUM & MASON
MAYFAIR
INDICA & SCOTCH OF ST. JAMES
PRINCESS DIANA MEMORIAL WALKWAY
Green Park
The Serpentine
HARD ROCK CAFE
ST. JAMES PALACE & CLARENCE HOUSE
GREEN PARK
ST JAMES PARK
Hyde Park Corner
Constitution Hill
Kensington Rd
Knightsbridge
BUCKINGHAM PALACE
Birdcage Walk
HARVEY NICHOLS
KNIGHTSBRIDGE
Knightsbridge
THE QUEEN'S GALLERY
HARRODS
THE ROYAL MEWS
BROMPTON
Victoria St
BELGRAVIA
Victoria Station
Sloane Square
CHELSEA KITCHEN
CHELSEA
RANALAGH GARDENS
PIMLICO

1/8   mile   1/4
N
◉ Underground stops
★ Featured sights
- - Princess Diana walk

156

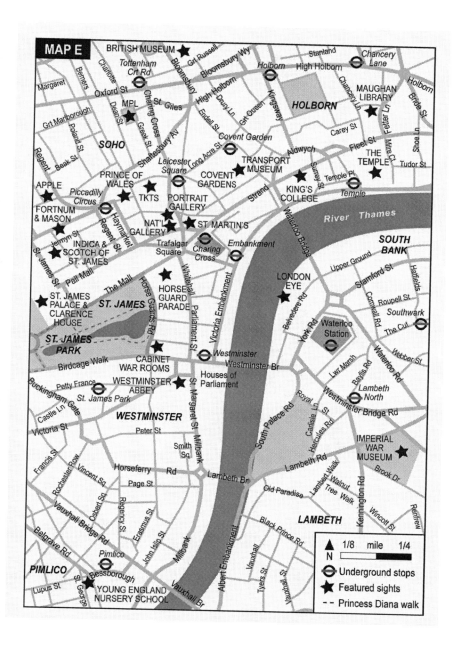

MAP E

BRITISH MUSEUM ★

Tottenham
Crt Rd

Margaret
Berners
Charlotte

Oxford St

Grt Marlborough
Poland St

Regent
Beak St

St. Giles

Dean St
Greek St
Shaftesbury Av

Bloomsbury
Grt Russell
High Holborn
Bloomsbury Wy

Drug Ln
Endell St
Long Acre St
Grt Queen
Kingsway

Stanland

Holborn   High Holborn

Chancery
Lane

HOLBORN

MAUGHAN
LIBRARY ★

Holborn

Bride St

MPL ★

Covent Garden

TRANSPORT
MUSEUM ★

Carey St

Chancery Ln

Fetter Ln

Shoe Ln

SOHO

Leicester
Square

COVENT
GARDENS

Aldwych

Strand

Temple Pl

Fleet St

THE
TEMPLE ★

Tudor St

APPLE
★

Piccadilly
Circus

FORTNUM
& MASON ★

Jermyn St
St James St

PRINCE OF
WALES ★

Haymarket
Regent

TKTS ★

PORTRAIT
GALLERY

NAT'L
GALLERY ★

INDICA &
SCOTCH OF
ST. JAMES

Pall Mall

★ ST. MARTIN'S

Trafalgar
Square

KING'S
COLLEGE

Surrey St

Temple

Charing
Cross

Embankment

Waterloo Bridge

River Thames

SOUTH
BANK

Upper Ground

Stamford St

Roupell St

Cornwall Rd

Hatfields

Southwark

The Cut

The Mall

Horse Guards Rd

HORSE
GUARD
PARADE

Whitehall

Parliament St

Victoria Embankment

LONDON
EYE ★

Belvedere Rd

York Rd

Waterloo
Station

Webber St

Waterloo Rd

ST. JAMES
PALACE &
CLARENCE
HOUSE ★

ST. JAMES

**ST. JAMES
PARK**

Birdcage Walk

Buckingham Gate

Petty France

St. James Park

CABINET
WAR ROOMS ★

WESTMINSTER
ABBEY ★

Westminster

Houses of
Parliament

Westminster Br

Lwr Marsh

Baylis Rd

Lambeth
North

Westminster Bridge Rd

Castle Ln

Victoria St

WESTMINSTER

Peter St

St Margaret St

Millbank

South Palace Rd

Royal St

Carlisle Ln

Hercules Rd

IMPERIAL
WAR
MUSEUM ★

Brook Dr

Renfrew

Francis St
Rochester Row
Vincent Sq
Gt Peter St

Smith
Sq.

Horseferry   Rd

Page St

Lambeth Br

Lambeth Rd

Old Paradise

Lambeth Walk
Walnut
Tree Walk

Kennington Rd

Wincott St

Belgrave Rd
Vauxhall Bridge Rd

Regency St
Erasmus St
John Islip St

Millbank

Black Prince Rd

LAMBETH

Pimlico

PIMLICO

Lupus St

St George

Bessborough

YOUNG ENGLAND
NURSERY SCHOOL ★

Vauxhall Br

Albert Embankment

Vauxhall

Tyers St

Vauxhall St

▲
N

1/8   mile   1/4

Underground stops

★ Featured sights

- - Princess Diana walk

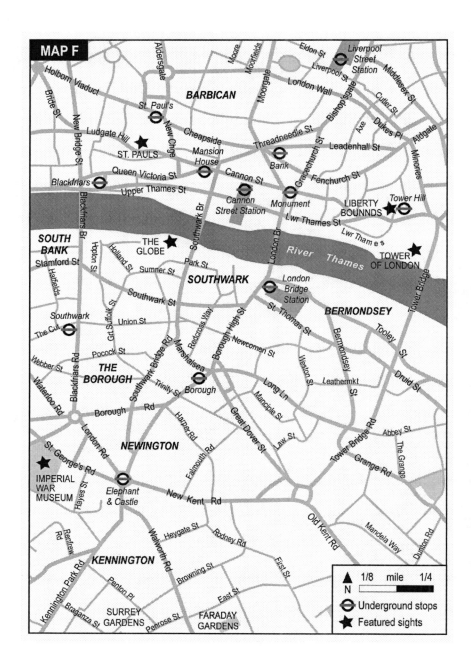

MAP F

Holborn Viaduct
Bride St
Aldersgate
Moorfields
Moorgate
Eldon St
Liverpool Street Station
Liverpool St
Middlesex St
Cutler St
Dukes Pl
Aldgate
Minories

BARBICAN

St. Paul's
New Chge
Cheapside
London Wall
Bishopsgate
Axe

★ ST. PAULS

Ludgate Hill
New Bridge St
Mansion House
Threadneedle St
Leadenhall St

Queen Victoria St
Bank
Gracechurch St
Fenchurch St

Blackfriars
Upper Thames St
Cannon St
Cannon Street Station
Monument
Lwr Thames St
LIBERTY BOUNNDS
Tower Hill ⬟
Lwr Thames

Blackfriars Br

SOUTH BANK
Stamford St
THE GLOBE ★
Southwark Br
Park St
London Br
River Thames
TOWER OF LONDON ★
Tower Bridge

Hopton St
Holland St
Sumner St
SOUTHWARK
London Bridge Station
BERMONDSEY

Hatfields
Southwark St
St. Thomas St
Tooley St
Druid St

Southwark
The Cut
Gt. Suffolk St
Union St
Redcross Way
Newcomen St
Bermondsey St
Leathermkt
Weston St

Webber St
Pocock St
Blackfriars Rd
THE BOROUGH
Southwark Bridge Rd
Marshalsea
Trinity St
Borough
Borough High St
Long Ln
Manciple St
Abbey St
The Grange

Waterloo Rd
Borough Rd
Harper Rd
Great Dover St
Law St
Tower Bridge Rd
Grange Rd

London Rd
St. George's Rd
NEWINGTON
Falmouth Rd

IMPERIAL WAR MUSEUM ★
Hayes St
Elephant & Castle
New Kent Rd
Old Kent Rd
Mandela Way
Dunton Rd

Renfrew Rd
Heygate St
Rodney Rd

KENNINGTON
Kennington Park Rd
Braganza St
Penton Pl
Walworth Rd
Browning St
East St
First St

SURREY GARDENS
Penrose St
FARADAY GARDENS

▲ N   1/8   mile   1/4

⊖ Underground stops

★ Featured sights

158

GENERAL INDEX